UNDERSTANDING
dBASE II

Grady Tate

UNDERSTANDING
dBASE II™

Alan Simpson

 Berkeley • Paris • Düsseldorf

Cover art by Jean-Francois Pénichoux
Book Design by Sharon Leong

dBASE II is a trademark of Ashton-Tate
CP/M, CBASIC, and CB-80 are registered trademarks of Digital Research Incorporated
MS-DOS and MBASIC are registered trademarks of Microsoft
WordStar and MailMerge are registered trademarks of MicroPro International
PC-DOS is a registered trademark of International Business Machines
SuperCalc is a registered trademark of Sorcim
Disk Doctor is a registered trademark of Super Soft
Quickcode is a registered trademark of Fox and Gellar
Microline is a registered trademark of Okidata Corporation

SYBEX is not affiliated with any manufacturer.

Library of Congress Card Number: 83-51202
ISBN 0-89588-147-0
Printed in the United States of America
10 9 8 7 6 5 4 3 2 1

To my parents,
Alan W. and Catherine Rose Simpson,
who made everything possible. Even probable.

Acknowledgements

This book, like most, was a team effort. It takes a lot of work to get a book from the idea stage to the shelves, and I'd like to thank those people who contributed their time, energy, and inspiration to the manuscript.

First and foremost is Carole Alden at SYBEX, my editor. Her long hours of work, patience with me, and fine editorial skill produced this book. She is actually more of a co-author than an editor. I'd like to thank Alan W. Simpson, my father, for his reviews of the original manuscript and tireless support. Thanks to William Gladstone, my agent, for getting me into the publishing business. Thank you Gloria Weir, for your unending support and enthusiasm.

And thanks to my students, who got the whole thing started in the first place.

Contents

APPENDICES

INTERFACING dBASE II WITH OTHER SOFTWARE SYSTEMS   221

GRAPHICS WITH dBASE II   233

C dBASE II Vocabulary   249

Introduction

dBASE II™ is a data base management system for microcomputers. This is a book about putting the computer to work for you using dBASE II. We will not be too concerned here about how the computer does it. This is a book about using the computer to our benefit. When we learn to drive a car, for example, we are not too concerned about the inner workings of the clutch or voltage regulator. Instead, we just want to get from point A to point B faster and more efficiently than walking. The same is true for the majority of computer users in the world today. Knowing about bits and bytes and B-trees is great, but most of us are more concerned about getting from A to B. Point A in the computer sense is doing dull tasks inefficiently, slowly, and with human error. Point B is letting the machine do dull tasks quickly, efficiently, and accurately.

This book is written with the computer novice in mind, but certainly more experienced users can learn from our examples too. The approach for teaching you to use dBASE focuses on the practical. Rather than just tell you what dBASE does, we show you with real-life everyday examples. We'll not only tell you what the dBASE commands mean, but we'll also teach you the concepts behind using the commands correctly. We'll also give you some good techniques for using dBASE II to its fullest potential.

If you have dBASE II handy, you should follow along by trying out the examples in the book. We assume that you are using a computer with two disk drives, drive A and drive B. The examples are set up such that dBASE II is on the disk in drive A, and the data bases we create are on the disk in drive B. You can use any disk configuration that you wish, however. For example, drive B is specified as the drive to put data bases on by preceding the filename with the symbol B: (i.e., CREATE B:MAIL, USE B:MAIL). If you don't have a drive B, just leave off the B: (i.e., CREATE MAIL, USE MAIL).

The contents of the book include the following. Chapters 1–7 deal with dBASE II basics: creating a data base; adding data to it; searching, sorting, and editing the data; and printing formatted reports. Chapters 8 and 9 deal with managing multiple data files, using an inventory system as the example. Chapters 10–16 discuss programming techniques which are used to go beyond the built-in capabilities of dBASE.

Appendix A discusses interfacing dBASE II with other programs such as WordStar, SuperCalc, and BASIC. Appendix B goes into graphics, and is basically just for fun. Appendix C is a summary of dBASE II commands that you can use as a reference.

What is a Data Base?

While *data base management* sounds so technical, it's as ordinary as driving a car. Think, for instance, of a shoe box full of index cards with names and addresses for a mailing list in it. The shoe box and its contents are a data base. Every time you juggle the index cards to get them in alphabetical order, you are *managing* the data base. The average office file cabinet is a data base too. It doesn't do anything, it just holds information (data). If you open a drawer and look up the Johnson account, you are searching your data base, a way of managing it.

We typically keep our everyday data bases in some order, either by alphabet, by date, or perhaps by zip code. We do so to *structure* our data base, so that it is easier for us to work with. We human data base managers do not like messy file cabinets. Ditto for computers. If we want to change the order of an alphabetical file, we might want to be able to say a magic word and have them instantly rearranged by zip code. Too bad we can't. Unfortunately, the task could take us hours of tedious labor. But with a computer, and the right magic word, the rearrangement can take place in seconds. But before we can discuss the magic words of dBASE II, we need to discuss a computer's view of a data base.

In the computer world, a data base is like our shoebox file, with a very rigid structure. While the shoe box is filled with index cards, a computer data base is filled with *records*. And while each index card in the shoe box may contain several written lines of information, a record in a data base contains *fields* of information. That is, a shoe box contains cards, each of which has several lines of information on it. A data base contains records, each of which has several fields within it. Take a look at the index card in Figure 1.1.

It has four lines of information on it: (1) name, (2) address, (3) city, state, zip, and (4) phone number. This single index card represents one record on a computer data base. Each of the lines roughly represents one field of information on the data base.

There is a very important difference between human data base managers and computer data base management systems. As people, we can tell what each line on the index card represents. That is, we know who this card refers to, his first and last name, as well as his address, city, state, zip code, and phone number. We know this

John Q. Smith
123 A. St.
San Diego, CA 92122

(619) 455-1212

Figure 1.1: Index card record

simply by looking at the context of the information. We can tell that (619) 455-1212 is not a last name. Though this is obvious to us, it is not at all clear to a computer. A computer can't tell a phone number from a last name from a pastrami sandwich. Unfortunately, the computer doesn't understand anything about information based on its context. Thus, we have to structure our data base rigidly so the computer does not mistake a name for a phone number, and we must be pretty explicit. Computers may be fast, but they are definitely not smart.

How do we structure a data base with dBASE II? First we have to decide exactly what we want to store. To do so, we have to break down the information on the index card into meaningful units of information. In the above example, one card holds a name, address, city, state, zip, and phone number. We will want each record in our data base to hold the same information. Recall that a given record on a data base refers to one index card in a shoe box, and that each field in a record refers to one piece of information on a given card. Hence, in our data base, we would want each record to contain:

NAME, ADDRESS, CITY, STATE, ZIP, PHONE

Notice that there are six fields on the record. Let me warn you here of the most common mistake that people make when structuring data bases. On the index card in Figure 1.1, we see four written lines: one contains the name, one contains the address, one contains the city, state and zip, and the other contains a phone number. Looking at the card, we might be tempted to structure the data base with these four fields:

NAME, ADDRESS, CSZ, PHONE

The CSZ field would contain the city, state and zip. This is misleading in reference to computer data bases because if we ever wanted to sort or search our data file by zip code, we couldn't. Since the zip would be combined with city and state, the computer couldn't isolate it. Thus, you should assign each single meaningful piece of information to a unique field. Therefore, this structure:

NAME, ADDRESS, CITY, STATE, ZIP, PHONE

is preferred, because each piece of data is placed in a separate field.

Learning to define meaningful items of information is an important aspect of data base management, as we shall see throughout this book. With the proper data base structure we can sort individuals by zip code, or search for individuals within a given zip code range. Because the zip code field is isolated from the city and state, it becomes a meaningful, individual piece of data for the computer to sort.

So then, how does the computer know what a given piece of information means? It doesn't. In the example above, we've told the computer that on each record, there are six fields. The first field is NAME, the second is ADDRESS, the third field is CITY, etc. If we store "John Q. Smith" in the ZIP field, the computer is not going to think about this and say to us, "That looks more like a name to me!" It will just store John Q. Smith as the zip code. Therefore, it is up to us to put the correct data in the appropriate field. We're the brains of the operation, not the computer.

Introduction to Data Base Management

Once we've structured our data base, we need to manage it by giving the computer precise instructions. Managing a data base primarily involves the following tasks:

1. ADD new data to the data base.

2. SORT the data base into some meaningful order.

3. SEARCH the data base for types of information.

4. PRINT data from our data base onto formatted reports.

5. EDIT data on the data base.

6. DELETE data from the data base.

We need to do similar tasks with our shoe box file. Occasionally we may need to add some new index cards. We may also want to sort the index cards into some meaningful order (say, alphabetically or by zip code). We might want to search through them and find all the people who live in Los Angeles, or all the people in the 92123 zip code area, or perhaps just find out where a person named Clark

Kenney lives. If Clark Kenney moves, we may want to edit the data base and change his address. Then again, if Clark Kenney stops paying his dues, we may want to delete him from the mailing list altogether. This is data base management. With the shoebox, we do all the work. With the computer, we think and the computer works.

Let's move on to Chapter 2 now and start talking about dBASE II more specifically.

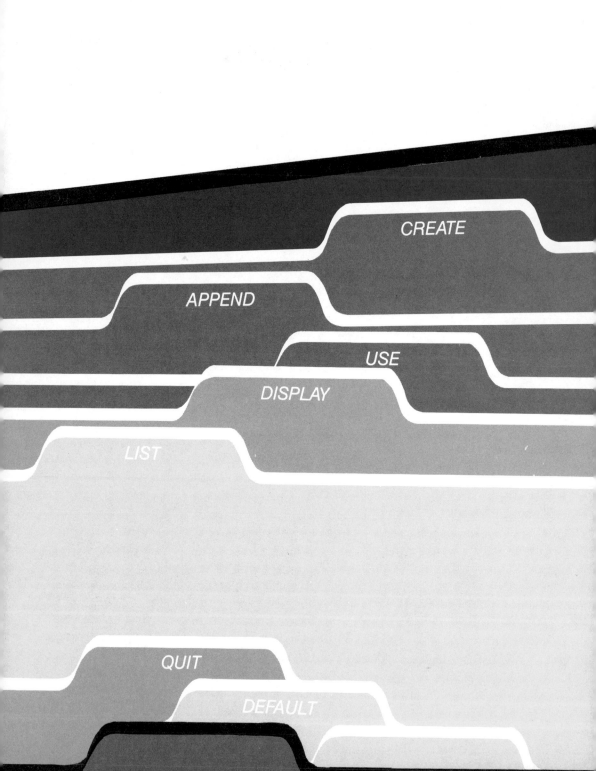

In this chapter, we'll learn to create a data base, add data to it, and retrieve data from it. If you have dBASE II readily available, we hope you'll load it up right now and follow every step of our examples. To load up your dBASE system, you need to place your dBASE II disk in drive A. If you have a drive B on your computer, put a blank, formatted disk in that drive. Then boot up so that the A> prompt appears on your screen. Next, type in DBASE and press the RETURN or ENTER key on the computer.

This will cause dBASE to load up and ask for today's date. We don't care about the date right now, so just press your RETURN key. This should bring up dBASE's dot prompt, which is a period (.) on the left-hand side of the screen. This tells you that dBASE is ready and waiting for instructions from you.

Creating a Data Base with CREATE

In order to create a data base, we need to type in the word CREATE next to the dBASE dot prompt, and press the RETURN key. When you see the symbol <RET> on these pages, it means "press the RETURN key." Do not type <RET> on the screen.
When we ask dBASE to CREATE a data base, it first asks us to

ENTER FILENAME:

Every data base must have a first and last name. You assign the first name, dBASE will add the last name .DBF (which stands for data base file). The name you assign can be up to eight characters long, without spaces or punctuation. For now, let's create a data base called MAIL. We can also specify the disk drive in the filename. If we place a B: in front of the file name, then the data base will be stored on the disk in drive B. So if you have a B drive with a disk in it, type in the filename like so:

   B:MAIL   <RET>

If you don't have a drive B, leave off the B:, and just type in the name MAIL <RET>.
Next, dBASE will want to know the structure of the data base. On the screen you'll see

ENTER RECORD STRUCTURE AS FOLLOWS:
FIELD   NAME,TYPE,WIDTH,DECIMAL PLACES
001

Let's discuss what all of this means. Notice that dBASE is asking for information about the fields in each record. For each field, it needs to know the name, type, width, and number of decimal places. The name of the field can be up to ten characters long, but no spaces are allowed, and the only punctuation allowed is a colon. dBASE also needs to know the type of data being stored in the field. Data can be one of three types: 1) character (C), for nonnumeric data such as name, address, etc.; 2) numeric (N), data for numbers that we want to do some math with, like dollar amounts or inventory quantity; 3) logical (L), where the field is either true or false. Then, dBASE needs to know the width of each field, the maximum number of characters that the field will contain. Finally, it needs to know how many decimal places are to be stored for numbers. For instance, in a dollar amount, we typically store two decimal places (i.e. $999.99).

Let's structure our MAIL data base like this:

```
ENTER RECORD STRUCTURE AS FOLLOWS:
FIELD    NAME,TYPE,WIDTH,DECIMAL PLACES
001      LNAME,C,15,0    <RET>
002      FNAME,C,10,0    <RET>
003      ADDRESS,C,25,0   <RET>
004      CITY,C,15,0    <RET>
005      STATE,C,5,0    <RET>
006      ZIP,C,10,0    <RET>
007      —    <RET>
```

Rather than typing in a seventh field, just press the RETURN key.

Notice that we've broken the first and last name into separate fields. The last name field (LNAME) can take a last name 15 letters long. The first name field (FNAME) can hold up to 10 letters.

Why are there two separate fields? Because in the future, we might want to sort our data alphabetically on last name. If we just had one field for both first and last name, such as Joe Smith, when we did our sort, dBASE would sort by first name. You and I can look at Joe Smith and immediately see that Smith is the last name. Since the computer doesn't understand this, we've established the difference between first and last name by providing a separate field for each. We've also put address, city, state, and zip into separate fields. Note that C indicates that each of these is a character field.

Now you'll probably ask, "Why is zip code a character string? Isn't 92122 a number?" Yes, it is, but hyphenated zip codes like 92038-2802 could cause problems. In dBASE, the hyphen means "subtract" when dealing with numbers. So at some point, 92038-2802 might become 89236 if stored as a number (92038 minus 2802 = 89236). This could wreak havoc on our mailing system.

Another problem is that some foreign zip codes have letters in them, like A132-09. In dBASE II, letters are not allowed in numeric data. We will save ourselves a lot of trouble by making zip a character field. The only time we must make a field numeric is when we need to do math. Certainly, we'll never need to total up zip codes!

So we now have a structured data base. All of our meaningful pieces of information are broken out into separate fields. Again, avoid the temptation to combine several pieces of information into one field (CITY:STATE:ZIP). dBASE II allows a maximum of 32 fields in each record, with their combined widths totalling up to a maximum of 1000 characters. There is plenty of room.

On your screen, you will now see that the computer is asking if we want to INPUT DATA NOW?. Type N for "no," and we will be returned to the dot prompt. There you have it. We have created a data base called MAIL.DBF on the disk in drive B.

If you are anything other than a perfect typist, you are likely to make a few typographical errors along the way. Computers are not forgiving of these, and dBASE will ask for a correction when you give it a command that it doesn't understand. For example, if while typing in the command, DISPLAY, you accidentally type in

DISMAY

dBASE will tell you

```
* * *UNKNOWN COMMAND
DISMAY
CORRECT AND RETRY (Y/N)?
```

to which you can reply by typing in the letter Y. dBASE will ask

CHANGE FROM:

and you can type in the letter M, then press the RETURN or ENTER key on your keyboard. dBASE will ask

CHANGE TO:

to which you can answer by typing in the letters PL and pressing the RETURN key. dBASE will show you the change and ask if there are more corrections to be made.

DISPLAY

MORE CORRECTIONS (Y/N)?

If your command looks OK, just answer "no" by typing in an N. dBASE will use the modified command.

Adding Data with APPEND

We've now got ourselves a nicely structured data base waiting to be filled. Let's start putting in some data. With the dBASE dot prompt showing, we are ready to let dBASE know what data base we will be referring to. The command for this is

USE B:MAIL   <RET>

The USE command tells dBASE which data base we will be working with. In the example above, we've told dBASE that we want to use the data base MAIL.DBF on the disk in drive B. dBASE promptly responds with another dot prompt. Now let's add some names and addresses to our data base.

The command for adding new data to a data base is APPEND. So, type in

APPEND   <RET>

This will bring us a form to fill out on the screen.

RECORD NUMBER: 00001

LNAME:_   :
FNAME: :
ADDRESS: :
CITY: :
STATE: :
ZIP: :

dBASE is now waiting for us to fill in the blanks. Here is the first can-
didate for our mailing list: John Q. Smith, 123 A. St., San Diego, CA,
92123. Notice that the cursor is waiting in the LNAME field. So, we
type Smith <RET>, John Q. <RET>, 123 A. St. <RET>, San
Diego <RET>, CA <RET> and 92123. Before pressing the last
<RET>, the screen will look like this:

RECORD NUMBER: 00001

LNAME:Smith   :
FNAME:John Q.   :
ADDRESS:123 A. St.   :
CITY:San Diego   :
STATE:CA   :
ZIP:92123_   :

We've filled in our first record. When we press <RET> after the zip
code, we get a new blank form.

RECORD NUMBER: 00002

LNAME:_   :
FNAME: :
ADDRESS: :
CITY: :
STATE: :
ZIP: :

Notice that dBASE is now waiting for the second record to be added
to the list (RECORD 00002). We can add as many names as we need
to. When you want to get out of the APPEND mode, just type
<RET> instead of typing in a last name. This will bring back the
dot prompt.

    If you need to correct mistakes while typing in data, there are sev-
eral *control-key* commands you can use. Some move the cursor and
some delete and insert information. The best way to learn these is to
try them. The symbol ^ means "hold down the control (CTRL) key
while typing." That is, ^E means hold down the CTRL key while you

press E. Here are the control-key commands:

^E   Moves cursor up 1 line.

^X   Moves cursor down 1 line.

^S   Moves cursor left 1 character.

^D   Moves cursor right 1 character.

^Y   Clears out data from this field.

^V   Inserts data into this field, rather than overwriting the data presently in the field. A second ^V turns the insert mode back off.

^G   Deletes the character in this cursor position.

Though the letters do not suggest the command they perform, they are assigned for a reason. All of them are in the left-hand portion of the keyboard, near the CTRL key. This is so that you can hold down the CTRL key with your little finger while pressing the appropriate key. The position of the keys suggest the direction that the cursor moves, as shown in Figure 2.1.

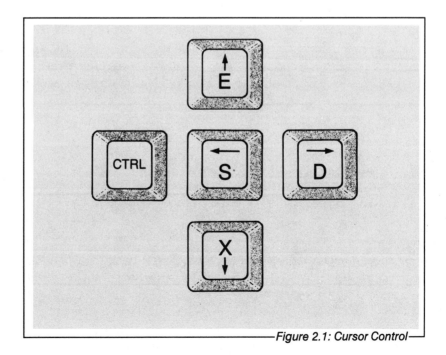

Figure 2.1: Cursor Control

These control-key commands hold true for most dBASE forms that appear on the screen.

Let's add a second record. Suppose that while adding our second record, we type in the following data:

```
RECORD NUMBER: 00002

LNAME:Appleby          :
FNAME:Andy       :
ADDRESS:35 Oak St.                :
CITY:Los Angeless     :
STATE:CA    :
ZIP:_          :
```

Before typing in the zip code we notice a couple of errors in the field above. To fix these, first, we can move the cursor up to the CITY field by holding down the CTRL key and tapping the E key twice. The cursor moves to the beginning of the CITY field like so:

```
CITY:Los Angeless     :
```

Now to move the cursor to the right, we hold down the CTRL key and tap the D key. If we do ten ^Ds, the cursor moves ten characters to the right. The cursor should now be under the first s in Angeless.

```
CITY:Los Angeless     :
```

We can delete the character above the cursor using a ^G. Now the city field looks like this:

```
CITY:Los Angeles     :
```

We've eliminated the extra s.

Next we notice that the address is supposed to be 345 Oak St., instead of 35 Oak St. We can do a ^E to move the cursor up to the ADDRESS field like so:

```
ADDRESS:35 Oak St.                :
```

Entering a ^D will move the cursor to the right one space, to here:

ADDRESS:3<u>5</u> Oak St.   :

Now we want to squeeze a 4 in between the 3 and the 5. To do so, we first have to go into an *insert mode*, by typing in a ^V. This puts the message INSERT on at the top of the screen. Now if we just type the number 4, the 4 is inserted between the 3 and the 5 like so:

ADDRESS:34<u>5</u> Oak St.   :

Now we can move back down to the zip field by typing in three ^Xs. Then we can type in a zip code (92123). Pressing <RET> after the zip code will then move us onto record 3 for appending.

So far so good. We've created a data base and added two records to it. At this point, if you are using dBASE, we suggest that you put in more data. If the APPEND form is still showing on the screen, just start keying in the following names and addresses. If the dBASE dot prompt is showing, just USE B:MAIL <RET> then type APPEND <RET>. Here are some data (records 3–6) for you to type in which we will use for future examples:

LNAME	FNAME	ADDRESS	CITY	STATE	ZIP
Smith	Dave	619 Elm St.	San Diego	CA	92122
SMITH	Betsy	222 Lemon Dr.	New York	NY	01234
Smithsonian	Lucy	461 Adams St.	San Diego	CA	92122-1234
Doe	Ruth	1142 J. St.	Los Angeles	CA	91234

After you type in the data for the last person on the list, dBASE will still ask for more data. To stop adding names, just press the RETURN key rather than typing in a last name. Once we get them all typed in, we need to learn ways to retrieve the information.

Viewing Data with DISPLAY and LIST

There are basically two commands for viewing the contents of a data base: the DISPLAY command, which displays the data of one record, and the LIST command, which displays all the records. Since DISPLAY has many other uses in dBASE, we are going to focus on the LIST command for now.

With dBASE's dot prompt showing, if we USE B:MAIL, we can view the contents of our data base by typing

　　LIST　　<RET>

This shows all of the data in our data base. Depending on how your particular screen handles overflows, you may see a messy screen. Mine came out looking like this:

```
00001   Smith        John Q.   123 A. St.        San Diego    CA
92123
00002   Appleby      Andy      345 Oak St.       Los Angeles  CA
92123
00003   Smith        Dave      619 Elm St.       San Diego    CA
92122
00004   SMITH        Betsy     222 Lemon Dr.     New York     NY
01234
00005   Smithsonian  Lucy      461 Adams St.     San Diego    CA
92122-1234
00006   Doe          Ruth      1142 J. St.       Los Angeles  CA
91234
```

The zip code for each record got stuck underneath each record number because the screen was not wide enough to handle the whole record. We can clean this up by requesting that only certain fields be listed. For example, the command

　　LIST LNAME,FNAME　　<RET>

gives us

```
00001   Smith         John Q.
00002   Appleby       Andy
00003   Smith         Dave
00004   SMITH         Betsy
00005   Smithsonian   Lucy
00006   Doe           Ruth
```

This is a cleaner display, with only the last and first name listed. We could reverse the order of first and last name by asking dBASE to

    LIST FNAME,LNAME   <RET>

which would give us

00001	John Q.	Smith
00002	Andy	Appleby
00003	Dave	Smith
00004	Betsy	SMITH
00005	Lucy	Smithsonian
00006	Ruth	Doe

The two fields are displayed in the order requested. We can ask for more information. Type in

    LIST FNAME,LNAME,ADDRESS,ZIP   <RET>

We will get exactly the information we request.

00001	John Q.	Smith	123 A. St.	92123
00002	Andy	Appleby	345 Oak St.	92123
00003	Dave	Smith	619 Elm St.	92122
00004	Betsy	SMITH	222 Lemon Dr.	01234
00005	Lucy	Smithsonian	461 Adams St.	92122-1234
00006	Ruth	Doe	1142 J. St.	91234

Now, try a few other types of LISTs. Be creative. Don't worry, you won't break or ruin anything.

When you finish a session with dBASE II, you should always type the command

    QUIT   <RET>

prior to removing any disks from their drives. This assures that all of your data will be safe and sound next time you wish to use dBASE II. The QUIT command returns you to the A> prompt, which is the safe time to remove disks from their drives. To get back into dBASE at a later date, just put the dBASE disk in drive A, and type DBASE <RET>next to the dot prompt.

We've come quite a way here. We can create a data base, add data to it, and display its contents. Quite the computer whizzes already. In the next chapter we'll learn how to search the data base for certain types of information. For example, suppose we only want to display people who live in Los Angeles, or in the 92122 zip code area. Perhaps we just want to look up a particular address. This is called *searching*.

NOTE: dBASE II allows you to change some general parameters using the SET command. In our examples in this book, we'll assume that none of these parameters have been altered. However, where appropriate, I'll mention how a parameter may affect an example. For instance, when creating and using our MAIL data base, we preceded the filename with a B: to tell dBASE that we wished to store this data base on the disk in drive B. Had we not put the B: in front, dBASE would have defaulted to the drive we booted up on, drive A. To set the default to drive B, you would need to type in the command

    SET DEFAULT TO B   <RET>

Once we set this parameter, dBASE will assume that the command to USE MAIL means USE B:MAIL. When you quit dBASE, all parameters are reset to their normal state. For the sake of consistency and clarity, we'll stick with the B:filename convention.

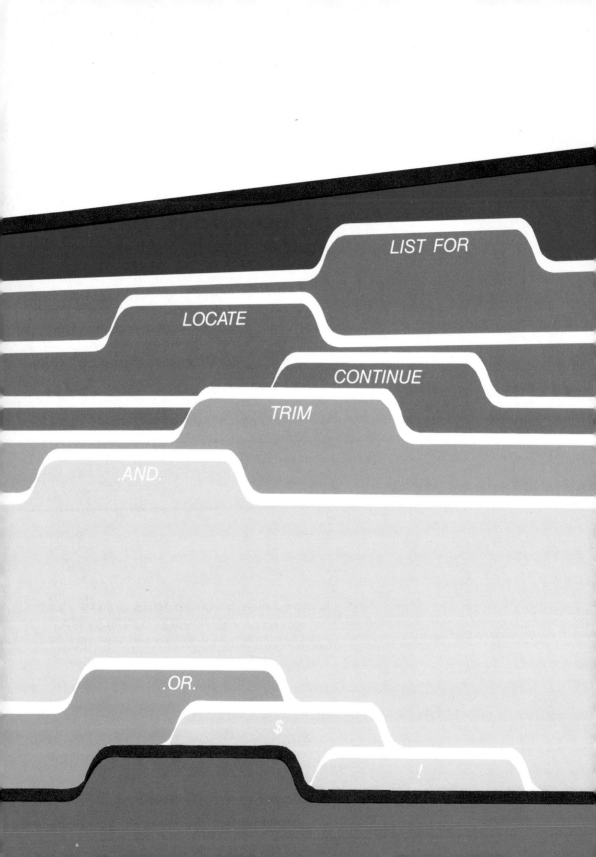

SEARCHING THE DATA BASE

3

In this chapter, we will be concerned with searching our data base for a particular record or records with certain characteristics in common. We'll use the LIST FOR and LOCATE commands.

Searching with LIST FOR

Let's dive in and start putting dBASE to work. Load up dBASE with the MAIL.DBF file in drive B. With the dBASE dot prompt showing, ask dBASE to

USE B:MAIL   <RET>

Let's begin with the LIST FOR command. Suppose we want a listing of people who live in the 92123 zip code area. We could type in the command

LIST FOR ZIP = '92123'   <RET>

Notice that we use the = to mean "equal to." The display would give us

```
00001   Smith     John Q.   123 A. St.   San Diego    CA   92123
00002   Appleby   Andy      345 Oak St.  Los Angeles  CA   92123
```

That is, all the people whose zip code = 92123. (From now on I'll cheat by making the LISTs fit the page, even though they might not fit the screen as shown.)

We can also display only certain fields, as usual, by specifying those fields in the LIST command. For example,

LIST FOR ZIP = '92123' LNAME,FNAME,ADDRESS,ZIP   <RET>

gives us a list with only the fields we've requested:

```
00001   Smith     John Q.   123 A. St.   92123
00002   Appleby   Andy      345 Oak St.  92123
```

You can also rearrange the order in which the fields are displayed. If you wanted to see the zip code on the left, you could type in

LIST FOR ZIP = '92123' ZIP,FNAME,LNAME,ADDRESS   <RET>

which would display

```
00001   92123   John Q.   Smith     123 A. St.
00002   92123   Andy      Appleby   345 Oak St.
```

Now the zip code is out in front. Suppose we need to find all the people on our list who live in Los Angeles. The command

    LIST FOR CITY = 'Los Angeles'   < RET >

would give us all Los Angeles residents.

00002	Appleby	Andy	345 Oak St.	Los Angeles	CA	92123
00006	Doe	Ruth	1142 J. St.	Los Angeles	CA	91234

    The numbers in the left-hand column are record numbers. That is, Andy Appleby is the second record of our data base, and Ruth Doe is the sixth record. The record number is useful for editing purposes, as we shall see later.

    If we need a list of everyone whose zip code is "greater than" 89999, we would use the following command:

    LIST FOR ZIP > '89999'   < RET >

So, our display would look like this:

00001	Smith	John Q.	123 A. St.	San Diego	CA	92123
00002	Appleby	Andy	345 Oak St.	Los Angeles	CA	92123
00003	Smith	Dave	619 Elm St.	San Diego	CA	92122
00005	Smithsonian	Lucy	461 Adams St.	San Diego	CA	92122-1234
00006	Doe	Ruth	1142 J. St.	Los Angeles	CA	91234

If we wanted to see a list of people whose zip code is "less than" 90000, we would ask dBASE to

    LIST FOR ZIP < '90000' ZIP,LNAME,FNAME,ADDRESS   < RET >

which would give us

00004	01234	SMITH	Betsy	222 Lemon Dr.	New York	NY

On our data base, Betsy Smith has the only zip code less than 90000. Her zip code is displayed in the column next to the record numbers because we asked for zip first in our field list.

    Notice that we always use the same order even though the commands are all different. We always say LIST FOR fieldname, operator, 'condition', plus things to list < RET >. This is the proper syntax for the LIST FOR command and any deviation from this may cause an error.

Would you like all of your information to fit on the screen? Try the TRIM function. (Whenever a ; ends a line, press < RET >.)

```
LIST TRIM(LNAME),TRIM(FNAME),TRIM(ADDRESS),;
     TRIM(CITY),STATE,ZIP    < RET >
```

Result:

```
00001    Smith John Q. 123 A. St. San Diego CA    92123
00002    Appleby Andy 345 Oak St. Los Angeles CA    92123
00003    Smith Dave 619 Elm St. San Diego CA    92122
00004    SMITH Betsy 222 Lemon Dr. New York NY    01234
00005    Smithsonian Lucy 461 Adams St. San Diego CA    92122-1234
00006    Doe Ruth 1142 J. St. Los Angeles CA    91234
```

dBASE pads the contents of every field with trailing blank spaces so that the information in each field forms vertical columns. The TRIM function will trim off these trailing blanks. Its syntax always requires parentheses, TRIM (field name).

Though the LIST command seems simple at first, you'll find some surprises. For example, if we want to find every Smith on our list, we would type

```
LIST FOR LNAME = 'Smith' LNAME, FNAME    < RET >
```

Result:

```
00001    Smith          John Q.
00003    Smith          Dave
00005    Smithsonian    Lucy
```

Hmmmm. There are a couple of problems here. First of all, Betsy SMITH is missing. Why? Because somebody typed in her last name as SMITH, instead of Smith. And Smith is not the same as SMITH from the computer's point of view. Second, what the heck is Smithsonian doing in there? We wanted Smiths, not everyone with Smith as the first five letters in their last name. Let's start solving these problems.

We can get rid of Smithsonian easily. Recall that dBASE pads all field data with blanks so that they fill in the field. In Chapter 2, we left 15 spaces for the last name field. So all the Smiths are actually "Smith_ _ _ _ _ _ _ _ _ _" as far as dBASE is concerned. We can omit Smithsonian in our display by specifying that only Smith, followed by a blank space, be displayed.

   LIST FOR LNAME = 'Smith ' LNAME, FNAME   < RET >

Now we see only the name Smith listed.

```
00001   Smith   John Q.
00003   Smith   Dave
```

Smithsonian didn't make it this time, because the first six letters of her last name are Smiths, not Smith_. Fooled the little devil. But we still have to deal with the absence of SMITH.

   The uppercase function (!) displays all lowercase letters in a character field in uppercase. We can test this out by typing in the command

   LIST !(LNAME)   < RET >

We then get

```
00001   SMITH
00002   APPLEBY
00003   SMITH
00004   SMITH
00005   SMITHSONIAN
00006   DOE
```

Here every last name on the list is displayed in uppercase. (They're still in upper- and lowercase on the data base though.) Now we can get dBASE to list all Smiths, ignoring upper- and lowercase by asking it to list all the people whose *uppercase equivalent* last name is SMITH. In dBASE, that looks like this:

   LIST FOR !(LNAME) = 'SMITH '   < RET >

In English, this statement reads, "List all the people whose last name, when translated to uppercase, is 'SMITH'."

Lo and behold, we get

00001	Smith	John Q.	123 A. St.	etc.
00003	Smith	Dave	619 Elm St.	etc.
00004	SMITH	Betsy	222 Lemon Dr.	etc.

We finally have the correct list. You really have to spell it out for these machines. They're so literal. They hardly ever do what you *mean*, they always do exactly what you *say*. No imagination! We got rid of Smithsonian here by listing for Smith followed by a blank space, and we got SMITH in by checking to see if the uppercase equivalent (!) of the last name was SMITH_.

Let's try another kind of list. Let's ask for a list of everybody except the Smiths by using the not equal to (#) sign.

> LIST FOR !(LNAME) # 'SMITH' LNAME,FNAME,ADDRESS   < RET >

We get

00002	Appleby	Andy	345 Oak St.
00006	Doe	Ruth	1142 J. St.

Here our list displays everyone whose last name is not Smith.

We've discussed the basics of LIST now. Let's talk about another type of searching.

Searching with the LOCATE Command

The LOCATE command is used for locating the position of a record based upon a desired characteristic. Since LOCATE does not display its data like LIST, we have to use the DISPLAY command along with it to see what dBASE has located. Like the LIST command, we use the FOR statement to indicate the characteristic we wish to find.

Let's assume we want dBASE to locate information on Dave Smith.

We could ask dBASE to search for Dave Smith by last name.

    LOCATE FOR LNAME = 'Smith'   < RET >

This would give us the dBASE display

RECORD 00001

This number doesn't do us much good. We can see the contents of the record by typing

    DISPLAY < RET >

We see this record displayed on the screen:

00001   Smith   John Q.   123 A. St.   San Diego   CA   92123

Whoops, this isn't Dave Smith. We can continue our search for Dave with the CONTINUE command. So type in

    CONTINUE   < RET >

which gives us

RECORD 00003

If we display this record by typing

    DISPLAY < RET >

we see that we have found Dave.

00003   Smith   Dave   619 Elm St.   San Diego   CA   92122

Not too bad, we got it in two tries. However, if we had 10,000 names on our mailing list, this process could take a long time. A quicker approach would be to ask for the desired record more specifically. To do this we use the .AND. operator.

    LOCATE FOR LNAME = 'Smith ' .AND. **FNAME** = 'Dave'   < RET >

Now, *two* statements must be true for LOCATE to find the correct record. That is, the last name must be Smith, *and* the first name must be Dave. The result of this command is

Record 00003

on the first shot. If we DISPLAY < RET > we see the following:

00003   Smith   Dave   619 Elm St.   San Diego   CA   92122

Got it in one try. If we type CONTINUE, we get

END OF FILE ENCOUNTERED

because dBASE has checked all other records and there is not another Dave Smith to be found.

Now, last but certainly not least, we will discuss the type of search where we need to know if a field roughly matches something we are looking for. For example, suppose we want to search for people living on a street named Lemon, no matter what the address number is or whether or not they live on Lemon St., Lemon Ave., or Lemon Blvd. If we LIST or LOCATE FOR ADDRESS = 'Lemon', no match will be found, because the word Lemon is embedded in the middle of the address field (i.e. 222 Lemon Dr.). We need some way to say, "Display all records that have the word Lemon embedded in the address field." That's quite a mouthful, but not in dBASE, because the $ function will find the embedded word. So, to locate an individual living on Lemon, we would use the command

    LOCATE FOR 'Lemon' $ADDRESS   < RET >

Notice that the grammar is reversed from what we've used before. This is because the $ means "embedded in." The syntax makes sense because the above command says, "Find a record with the word Lemon embedded in the address field." When we do the above command, we see on our screen

RECORD 00004

If we then

    DISPLAY   < RET >

we see

00004   SMITH   Betsy   222 Lemon Dr.   New York   NY   01234

Pretty good! It found a person living on Lemon. Keep in mind that any of the search examples we've shown with the LOCATE command work as well with the LIST command, and vice versa. That is, we could also LIST FOR 'Lemon' $ADDRESS. With this command, all individuals who live on Lemon would be displayed on the screen.

We can also combine search conditions to our heart's content. For example, if we want a listing of everyone who lives on either Elm or Oak streets, we could

LIST FOR 'Elm' $ADDRESS .OR. 'Oak' $ADDRESS   < RET >

which would give us

```
00002   Appleby   Andy   345 Oak St.   Los Angeles   CA   92123
00003   Smith     Dave   619 Elm St.   San Diego     CA   92122
```

The result is a listing of the individuals who live on either Oak or Elm streets. Be careful to distinguish *and* and *or*, though. If we had asked for a LIST FOR 'Elm' $ADDRESS .AND. 'OAK' $ADDRESS we would end up with nothing, because a given individual in our data base can't possibly live on both Elm and Oak Streets at the same time (unless he did happen to live at 3421 OakElm St.).

In summary, the .OR. operator requires that only one of the conditions has to be true to get a listing. The .AND. command requires that both search conditions be true. For instance, the command

LIST FOR 'Elm' $ADDRESS .AND. 'San Diego' $CITY   < RET >

would tell dBASE to display all of the individuals who live on Elm St. *and* in San Diego (San Diego residents who live on Elm). The command

LIST FOR 'Elm' $ADDRESS .OR. 'San Diego' $CITY   < RET >

would display all individuals living on Elm St., regardless of what city, and all people living in San Diego, regardless of what street. The .OR. command generally broadens a search, since only one condition out of two must be met for dBASE to bring the data to the screen. On the other hand, the .AND. function narrows the search, since both search conditions must be met to find the correct data.

We can combine .AND. and .OR. search conditions. Try the following command:

```
LIST FOR STATE = 'CA' .AND. ('Oak' $ADDRESS .OR. 'Elm'
    $ADDRESS)
```

This command would first require that the individual live in California. Furthermore, the individual must live on either Oak or Elm to make it to the list. In other words, this command lists all California residents who live on either Oak or Elm.

Well, perhaps we're getting carried away here. We could spend 1000 more pages discussing search possibilities, but it's better to experiment with a few searches of your own. Experience is the best teacher when it comes to computers. Don't be intimidated by errors, because they only teach you how to avoid them in the future.

In the next chapter, we will discuss dBASE commands for sorting records into some meaningful order.

NOTE: In the searching examples, I stated that a LIST or LOCATE for LNAME = 'Smith' would display Smithsonian also, since Smith represents the first five letters of Smithsonian. I suggested using 'LIST FOR LNAME = 'Smith ' (Smith followed by a blank space) to make the search more exact. There is another way to achieve the same effect. dBASE has a built-in 'EXACT' parameter which, unless specifically requested, is in the OFF mode. We can turn it on by typing in the command

```
SET EXACT ON    <RET>
```

next to the dot prompt. This changes the results of the search to only those cases where the match is exact. Hence, if I had first SET EXACT ON, then requested a LIST FOR LNAME = 'Smith', Smithsonian would not have shown up, since this is not an EXACT match.

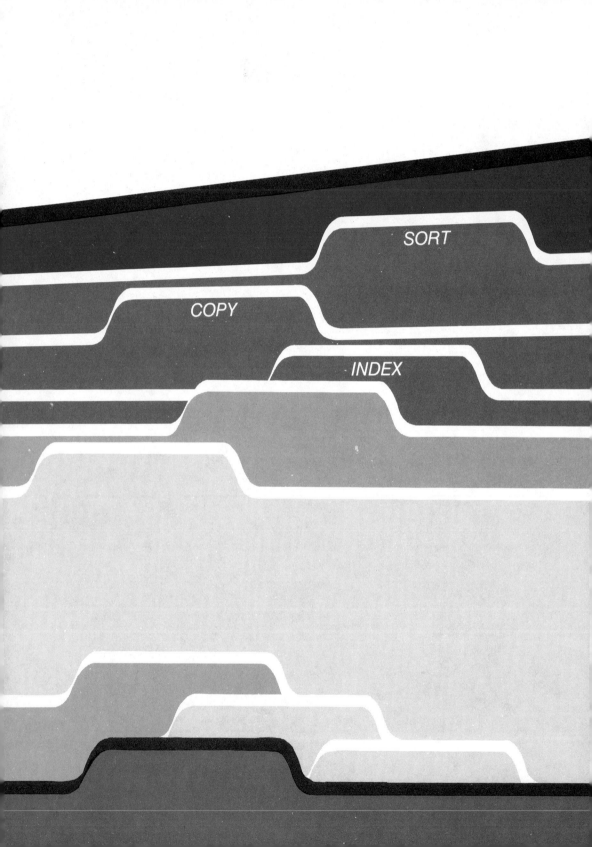

SORTING THE DATA BASE

4

In most situations we add new data to our data base as they become available to us. Then, at some point, we need to rearrange the records into some meaningful order, such as by zip code for bulk mailing, or by last name for a directory. dBASE provides two commands for sorting our data bases, SORT and INDEX. We'll discuss each command individually below.

Sorting with SORT

When we use the SORT command to sort our files, dBASE requires that we create a new data base to store the sorted records on. Once the sorting is done, we can COPY the contents of the sorted data base back into the original file. Let's try an alphabetical sort with our MAIL file on drive B. When we SORT, we'll store the newly arranged data to a file called TEMP (for temporary) on drive B (B:TEMP). After dBASE sorts the data we will copy the contents of B:TEMP back over to B:MAIL, so that the records in B:MAIL will be properly sorted.

OK, here we go. First, we want to be sure to USE B:MAIL. Take a quick look at its current state with a LIST command. You will see

00001	Smith	John Q.	123 A. St.	San Diego	CA	92123
00002	Appleby	Andy	345 Oak St.	Los Angeles	CA	92123
00003	Smith	Dave	619 Elm St.	San Diego	CA	92122
00004	SMITH	Betsy	222 Lemon Dr.	New York	NY	01234
00005	Smithsonian	Lucy	461 Adams St.	San Diego	CA	92122-1234
00006	Doe	Ruth	1142 J. St.	Los Angeles	CA	91234

Now, let's

SORT ON LNAME TO B:TEMP   <RET>

After the disk drives whir and buzz for a while, dBASE tells us that

SORT COMPLETE

Eagerly, we type LIST <RET> and again we see

00001	Smith	John Q.	123 A. St.	San Diego	CA	92123
00002	Appleby	Andy	345 Oak St.	Los Angeles	CA	92123
00003	Smith	Dave	619 Elm St.	San Diego	CA	92122
00004	SMITH	Betsy	222 Lemon Dr.	New York	NY	01234
00005	Smithsonian	Lucy	461 Adams St.	San Diego	CA	92122-1234
00006	Doe	Ruth	1142 J. St.	Los Angeles	CA	91234

What? These records don't look sorted to me. That's because we are listing for B:MAIL again. Remember, we sorted to B:TEMP. The sorted records are in the file B:TEMP. So, let's USE B:TEMP <RET>. Now, if we LIST, we see our sorted records.

00001	Appleby	Andy	345 Oak St.	Los Angeles	CA	92123
00002	Doe	Ruth	1142 J. St.	Los Angeles	CA	91234
00003	SMITH	Betsy	222 Lemon Dr.	New York	NY	01234
00004	Smith	John Q.	123 A. St.	San Diego	CA	92123
00005	Smith	Dave	619 Elm St.	San Diego	CA	92122
00006	Smithsonian	Lucy	461 Adams St.	San Diego	CA	92122-1234

Fine and dandy. So B:TEMP has the sorted records on it, but our MAIL data base is still in random order. How do we put the sorted contents of B:TEMP into B:MAIL? Simple. Since B:TEMP is in use, we can just

COPY TO B:MAIL   <RET>

dBASE informs us that

00006 RECORDS COPIED

Now if we use B:MAIL, and do a LIST, we see

00001	Appleby	Andy	345 Oak St.	Los Angeles	CA	92123
00002	Doe	Ruth	1142 J. St.	Los Angeles	CA	91234
00003	SMITH	Betsy	222 Lemon Dr.	New York	NY	01234
00004	Smith	John Q.	123 A. St.	San Diego	CA	92123
00005	Smith	Dave	619 Elm St.	San Diego	CA	92122
00006	Smithsonian	Lucy	461 Adams St.	San Diego	CA	92122-1234

We have everything in alphabetical order now.

Let's illustrate what took place on the diskette in drive B with some pictures. To start with, the disk in drive B had a data base called MAIL on it, with the records in random order (the order in which they were entered). Figure 4.1 shows the contents of our disk.

dBASE requires that when we SORT the data base, we must sort *to* another data file. In our example, we sorted to a data base called B:TEMP. After the sort was complete, we had two data bases on the disk: MAIL.DBF, still in random order, and TEMP.DBF, which had the same contents as MAIL.DBF, but in sorted order, as in Figure 4.2.

In order to see the names and addresses in sorted order, we needed to USE B:TEMP, then LIST the records. However, we wanted the data on MAIL to be sorted too, so we used the COPY command to copy the sorted contents of TEMP over to MAIL. After the sort was complete, we had two identical data bases, as shown in Figure 4.3.

We don't actually need the TEMP file anymore; we just needed it to temporarily hold the sorted records. We'll discuss techniques for deleting unnecessary data files in the next chapter.

Now suppose we want to do a bulk mailing, and we need these little charmers in zip code order, what do we do? I bet you can guess.

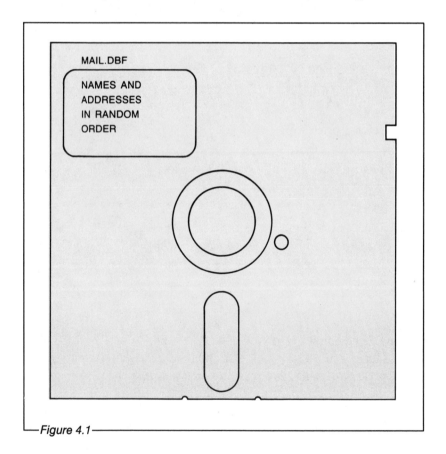

MAIL.DBF

NAMES AND
ADDRESSES
IN RANDOM
ORDER

Figure 4.1

SORT ON ZIP TO B:TEMP   < RET>

Now, we'll USE B:TEMP, from there COPY TO B:MAIL, then USE B:MAIL. Doing a LIST we get

00001	SMITH	Betsy	222 Lemon Dr.	New York	NY	01234
00002	Doe	Ruth	1142 J. St.	Los Angeles	CA	91234
00003	Smith	Dave	619 Elm St.	San Diego	CA	92122
00004	Smithsonian	Lucy	461 Adams St.	San Diego	CA	92122-1234
00005	Appleby	Andy	345 Oak St.	Los Angeles	CA	92123
00006	Smith	John Q.	123 A. St.	San Diego	CA	92123

The records are now in zip code order, from smallest to largest. You say you want your zip codes to go from largest to smallest instead?

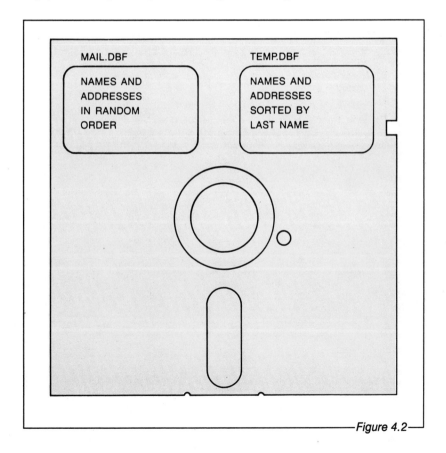

MAIL.DBF

NAMES AND
ADDRESSES
IN RANDOM
ORDER

TEMP.DBF

NAMES AND
ADDRESSES
SORTED BY
LAST NAME

Figure 4.2

Who am I to question why? Easier just to:

SORT ON ZIP TO B:TEMP DESCENDING   <RET>

When we see

SORT COMPLETE

we just

USE B:TEMP   <RET>   (wait for dot prompt to
                           reappear after each command)
COPY TO B:MAIL   <RET>
USE B:MAIL   <RET>
LIST   <RET>

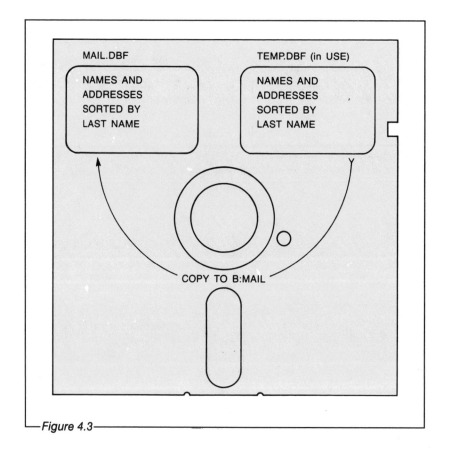

MAIL.DBF   TEMP.DBF (in USE)

NAMES AND   NAMES AND
ADDRESSES   ADDRESSES
SORTED BY   SORTED BY
LAST NAME   LAST NAME

COPY TO B:MAIL

Figure 4.3

and get the following:

00001	Appleby	Andy	345 Oak St.	Los Angeles	CA	92123
00002	Smith	John Q.	123 A. St.	San Diego	CA	92123
00003	Smithsonian	Lucy	461 Adams St.	San Diego	CA	92122-1234
00004	Smith	Dave	619 Elm St.	San Diego	CA	92122
00005	Doe	Ruth	1142 J. St.	Los Angeles	CA	91234
00006	SMITH	Betsy	222 Lemon Dr.	New York	NY	01234

The records are now in zip code order from largest to smallest, because we specified that we wanted the SORT done in *descending* order.

Sorting in this fashion is useful, but there are disadvantages. First, sorting wastes disk space. Since dBASE does the sorting to another data base file, we need at least as much empty space on the disk as the data base itself fills. That means we can only use half a disk for our entire data base since we need the other half to SORT TO. Second, sorting is quite slow. You may not think so with this little data base, but you would if you had 5000 records. This can be especially painful when you want them sorted by name for a directory, sorted by zip code for mailings, and so forth. Also, since everyone's record number changes as the records become rearranged, we can never be sure of an individual's record number using the SORT command. This last disadvantage may seem trivial now, but with large data bases, it's nice to have record numbers remain constant. What is the solution to these problems? The INDEX command is.

Sorting with INDEX

The INDEX command provides us with a much quicker and more efficient method of sorting records than does the SORT command. The command grammar is similar to the SORT command's grammar, but the approach is altogether different. Let's use the INDEX command to sort on last names. We will use a file called NAMES to do our indexing.

INDEX ON LNAME TO B:NAMES   <RET>

When we do a LIST, we see displayed on the screen

00001	Appleby	Andy	345 Oak St.	Los Angeles	CA	92123
00005	Doe	Ruth	1142 J. St.	Los Angeles	CA	91234
00006	SMITH	Betsy	222 Lemon Dr.	New York	NY	01234
00002	Smith	John Q.	123 A. St.	San Diego	CA	92123
00004	Smith	Dave	619 Elm St.	San Diego	CA	92122
00003	Smithsonian	Lucy	461 Adams St.	San Diego	CA	92122-1234

The records have changed to proper order, but the record numbers have remained the same. This is helpful, because that means Andy Appleby is still record 2, Ruth Doe is still record 6, etc. Also, we didn't have to go through the COPY TO rigamarole to see the records listed in proper order.

In our command, we asked dBASE to INDEX to B:NAMES. Isn't B:NAMES a data file? Yes, but it is not a data base. It is a special file, an *index file* named NAMES.NDX. Its contents look very much like an index in a book. A book's index has a list of keywords in alphabetical order, and page numbers where the keywords appear in text. Our data base index has a list of last names in alphabetical order, and the record numbers where they appear on the data base, like so:

Appleby	00001
Doe	00005
SMITH	00006
Smith	00002
Smith	00004
Smithsonian	00003

After the index is complete, when we LIST, dBASE automatically uses information from the index file to determine the proper order to display the records in MAIL.DBF. The records in the MAIL.DBF data base are still in their original order; the index file, however, tells dBASE the proper order in which to display the records.

After we do an index, the MAIL.DBF and NAMES.NDX files exist on the disk, as in Figure 4.4.

Let's try another example. This time we'll index on the ZIP field. First, we'll

   USE B:MAIL   < RET >

then

   INDEX ON ZIP TO B:ZIP   < RET >

Doing a LIST, we see

00006	SMITH	Betsy	222 Lemon Dr.	New York	NY	01234
00005	Doe	Ruth	1142 J. St.	Los Angeles	CA	91234
00004	Smith	Dave	619 Elm St.	San Diego	CA	92122
00003	Smithsonian	Lucy	461 Adams St.	San Diego	CA	92122-1234
00001	Appleby	Andy	345 Oak St.	Los Angeles	CA	92123
00002	Smith	John Q.	123 A. St.	San Diego	CA	92123

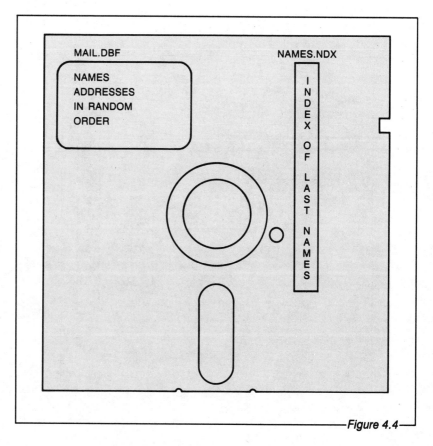

MAIL.DBF

NAMES
ADDRESSES
IN RANDOM
ORDER

NAMES.NDX

INDEX OF LAST NAMES

Figure 4.4

The records are now displayed in zip code order. Furthermore, we have a file on drive B called ZIP.NDX which tells dBASE the order in which to display records, as in Figure 4.5.

Now here is the real beauty of indexing. If we want a quick view of our mailing list sorted alphabetically by name, we don't have to sort it again. We just tell dBASE to

USE B:MAIL INDEX B:NAMES   <RET>

then LIST <RET>, which gives us

00001	Appleby	Andy	345 Oak St.	Los Angeles	CA	92123
00005	Doe	Ruth	1142 J. St.	Los Angeles	CA	91234
00006	SMITH	Betsy	222 Lemon Dr.	New York	NY	01234
00002	Smith	John Q.	123 A. St.	San Diego	CA	92123
00004	Smith	Dave	619 Elm St.	San Diego	CA	92122
00003	Smithsonian	Lucy	461 Adams St.	San Diego	CA	92122-1234

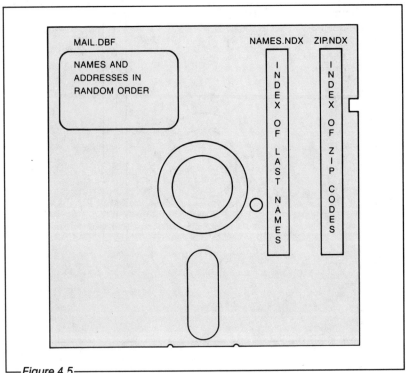

Figure 4.5

When we want a quick look at our mailing list in zip code order we don't have to re-sort anything since we've already indexed on zip, and ZIP.NDX still exists. We just tell dBASE to

USE B:MAIL INDEX B:ZIP   <RET>

then LIST <RET> immediately gives us

00004	SMITH	Betsy	222 Lemon Dr.	New York	NY	01234
00006	Doe	Ruth	1142 J. St.	Los Angeles	CA	91234
00003	Smith	Dave	619 Elm St.	San Diego	CA	92122
00005	Smithsonian	Lucy	461 Adams St.	San Diego	CA	92122-1234
00002	Appleby	Andy	345 Oak St.	Los Angeles	CA	92123
00001	Smith	John Q.	123 A. St.	San Diego	CA	92123

Furthermore, an index (.NDX) file takes up much less disk space than a SORT TO file, so we don't have to worry about reserving half of a disk's capacity for the SORT TO file. The INDEX command does everything that the SORT command does, but faster and better. I encourage you to use the INDEX command rather than the SORT command. Just practice a little with it; you'll get the hang of it in no time.

Sorts within Sorts

Let's take a look at our B:MAIL file indexed by LNAME. That is, let's USE B:MAIL INDEX B:NAMES, then LIST the file. We see

00002	Appleby	Andy	345 Oak St.	Los Angeles	CA	92123
00006	Doe	Ruth	1142 J. St.	Los Angeles	CA	91234
00004	SMITH	Betsy	222 Lemon Dr.	New York	NY	01234
00001	Smith	John Q.	123 A. St.	San Diego	CA	92123
00003	Smith	Dave	619 Elm St.	San Diego	CA	92122
00005	Smithsonian	Lucy	461 Adams St.	San Diego	CA	92122-1234

It is sorted on last names, but if we look closely at all the Smiths, we can see that the first names are not alphabetized. That is, John Smith comes before Dave Smith. To really shape up this data base, we want to SORT (or INDEX) by last name, and then within each last name, sort by first name, so that Dave Smith comes before John Smith. "Ahaa!" you say, "Do two sorts!" Sorry, it doesn't work that way. We need to do one sort on two separate fields. That is, we need to

> INDEX ON LNAME + FNAME TO B:BOTH   <RET>

If we now LIST <RET> the records are displayed in the requested order.

00002	Appleby	Andy	345 Oak St.	Los Angeles	CA	92123
00006	Doe	Ruth	1142 J. St.	Los Angeles	CA	91234
00004	SMITH	Betsy	222 Lemon Dr.	New York	NY	01234
00003	Smith	Dave	619 Elm St.	San Diego	CA	92122
00001	Smith	John Q.	123 A. St.	San Diego	CA	92123
00005	Smithsonian	Lucy	461 Adams St.	San Diego	CA	92122-1234

John Smith is now properly placed after Dave Smith. In our INDEX command line, we've told dBASE to index on last name, and to index on first name within the last names. That was easy.

Now suppose we want the records sorted by zip code, and within each zip code batch, we want the names in alphabetical order. Easy enough. We would just ask dBASE to index on zip code as the primary sort order, and last name as the secondary sort order. How do we say that in dBASE?

> INDEX ON ZIP + LNAME TO B:ZNAMES   <RET>

If you don't like ZNAMES, use any filename you like. Either way, the records will be sorted by zip code, and within each zip code batch, names will appear in alphabetical order by last name. After typing it in, we then

> LIST   <RET>

Our file is sorted as we asked.

00006	SMITH	Betsy	222 Lemon Dr.	New York	NY	01234
00005	Doe	Ruth	1142 J. St.	Los Angeles	CA	91234
00004	Smith	Dave	619 Elm St.	San Diego	CA	92122
00003	Smithsonian	Lucy	461 Adams St.	San Diego	CA	92122-1234
00001	Appleby	Andy	345 Oak St.	Los Angeles	CA	92123
00002	Smith	John Q.	123 A. St.	San Diego	CA	92123

We can see the ordering more clearly if we just list the zip code and last name fields, like so:

LIST ZIP,LNAME   < RET >

The response is

00006	01234	SMITH
00005	91234	Doe
00004	92122	Smith
00003	92122-1234	Smithsonian
00001	92123	Appleby
00002	92123	Smith

Within the common 92123 zip codes near the bottom of the list, the last names are alphabetized. Piece o' cake. But, we still only have the last names sorted within each zip code batch. If we had a very large data base, it might behoove us to sort by zip code, alphabetically by last name within each zip code batch, and alphabetically by first name within common last names. This sounds complicated, but we just have to ask dBASE to index on the three fields:

INDEX ON ZIP + LNAME + FNAME TO B:ALL   < RET >

and our wish comes true. When you USE B:MAIL INDEX B:ALL, your mailing list would appear in zip code order, with last names alphabetized within each zip code batch, and first names alphabetized within each last name. Our present B:MAIL data base is too small to demonstrate this. But trust me, it works.

There are some techniques you can use to manage multiple index files. These are discussed in Chapter 17.

Now I want to fill you in on a little trick I learned while managing my own mailing list system. I was concerned about the size of it, so I thought I'd check to see if there were any duplicate street addresses on the data base. I didn't feel like writing an elaborate program to do this, so I decided to

```
USE B:MAIL   <RET>
INDEX ON B:ADDRESS TO B:STREETS   <RET>
```

When I got the dot prompt, I just asked for a list of addresses, last names, first names, and cities. That is, I asked dBASE to

```
LIST ADDRESS,LNAME,FNAME,CITY   <RET>
```

and I got this:

00009	123 A. St.	Jones	John	San Diego
00097	123 A. St.	Jones	John	San Diego
00321	1291 Adams Ave.	Smith	Robert	Los Angeles
00932	1300 Curie Way	Bragg	Andy	San Diego
01943	1410 Pacific Dr.	Quinn	Mary	Los Angeles
00032	1410 Pacific Dr.	Gorton	John	Los Angeles
00761	1492 Ingraham St.	Hammer	Fanny	San Diego
00007	1510 Metropolis Rd.	Kenney	Clark	Metropolis

Running my finger down the address column, I could see that 123 A. St. appeared twice on my mailing list, in both record 9 and record 97. Furthermore, I could see that two people at 1410 Pacific Dr. were getting mail from me. I decided to delete the second occurrence of John Jones from the data base. I also decided that I'd call one of the folks at 1410 Pacific Drive and ask if they really needed two mailings.

Hmmm. We didn't think to put phone numbers on our data base. Even though we wouldn't need them for mailings, they could come in handy at other times. We'll discuss techniques for adding new fields to an existing data base in the next chapter, as well as techniques for editing and deleting data.

EDIT

BROWSE

CHANGE

REPLACE

DELETE

PACK

RECALL

APPEND FROM   MODIFY STRUCTURE

EDITING AND MODIFYING DATA BASES

5

When working with computers, the term *edit* means to change existing data on the data base. For instance, if a certain individual who is already on our data base moves to a new house, we would want to change his street address. That would be a data base edit. Suppose we decide that we want to include phone numbers for each individual on our data base, even though we did not originally designate a field for storing phone numbers. We would have to modify the structure of the data base. The commands we can use to perform such feats are discussed in this chapter.

Editing with EDIT

Computer data bases need editing for a variety of reasons. People move and change their addresses, we make mistakes while entering data and have to fix them, and so forth. Editing with dBASE is a rather simple task if we know the number of the particular record we are looking for. We can't possibly remember all those numbers, but we can use the knowledge we've gained thus far to quickly look up a record number.

Let's suppose that Dave Smith from our MAIL data base moves and we need to change his address. We have no idea what Dave's record number is, so we set out to find it. This is not difficult. We just load up dBASE, and

> **USE B:MAIL   <RET>**

Then we

> **LIST FOR LNAME = 'Smith ' .AND. FNAME = 'Dave'   <RET>**

This would give us the following display on the screen:

00004   Smith   Dave   619 Elm St.   San Diego   CA   92122

dBASE informs us that we have only one Dave Smith, and his record number is 00004. Of course, if we had many Dave Smiths on our data base, we might have to pick out the appropriate one from the display based on context. But for this example, suffice it to say that we've located our Dave Smith. He is record 4, as the left-most column informs us. Now, to change Dave's data, we type

> **EDIT 4   <RET>**

next to the dBASE dot prompt. This gives us a new form to fill out which looks like this on our screen:

RECORD 00004

```
LNAME     :Smith            :
FNAME     :Dave       :
ADDRESS :619 Elm St.              :
CITY       :San Diego        :
STATE     :CA    :
ZIP         :92122        :
```

Notice that the cursor is under the first letter of Smith. Now, we can use control-key commands to move the cursor around and fill in new data. Remember, the ^ symbol means "hold down the CTRL key while pressing the letter key." Control-key commands for the EDIT mode are:

^E   Moves cursor up 1 line.

^X   Moves cursor down 1 line.

^S   Moves cursor left 1 character.

^D   Moves cursor right 1 character.

^V   Turns insert mode on/off.

^G   Deletes character over cursor.

^Y   Clears out this field.

^W   Saves data as they appear on screen and returns to dot prompt.

^R   Saves data as they appear on screen and goes to previous record.

^C   Saves data as they appear on screen and goes to next record.

^Q   Abandons edited data and restores original values.

^U   Marks this record for deletion, or unmarks if already marked.

To change Dave's address here, we type a ^XX to move the cursor down two lines. This positions the cursor at the front of the address field. A ^Y now will empty out the ADDRESS field, and we can type in 123 B. St. We can then drop down another line (^X), clear out the present city (^Y), and type in Los Angeles. Two more ^Xs will put us in the zip field, where we can change the zip code to read 90123. Now Dave Smith's data looks like this:

```
RECORD 00004

LNAME     :Smith          :
FNAME     :Dave      :
ADDRESS :123 B. St.               :
CITY        :Los Angeles   :
STATE      :CA    :
ZIP         :90123_     :
```

At this point, it is important that we check to see if the data looks ok. If it does, we next save the new data by pressing a ^W. This will bring us back to the dot prompt.

If you practice using the edit mode, you will find it easy to use. It is a straightforward procedure; there is nothing particularly tricky about it. At this point, you can try editing a few records of your own.

Editing with BROWSE

The dBASE II user's manual states that the BROWSE command must be seen to be appreciated. This is true, especially with a very large data base. The BROWSE command allows us to scroll through the data base, both horizontally and vertically. As we pan, dBASE shows as much data as will fit on the screen. We can move the cursor to change whatever information we please. This is a very useful technique for locating obvious errors, like misspellings, that can be easily corrected. To enter the BROWSE mode, we simply type in the command

BROWSE   <RET>

The screen then displays as much information as will fit. The BROWSE display looks something like this:

RECORD NUMBER: 00001

LNAME	FNAME	ADDRESS	CITY
Smith	John Q.	123 A. St.	San Diego
Appleby	Andy	345 Oak St.	Los Angeles
Smith	Dave	123 B. St.	Los Angeles
SMITH	Betsy	222 Lemon Dr.	New York
Smithsonian	Lucy	461 Adams St.	San Diego
Doe	Ruth	1142 J. St.	Los Angeles

Now we can move the cursor to alter whatever information we like. The control-key commands used with the BROWSE command are:

^E   Moves cursor left 1 field, or up 1 line (if no more fields to the left).

^X   Moves cursor right 1 field, or down 1 line (if no more fields to the right).

^D   Moves cursor right 1 space.

^S   Moves cursor left 1 space.

^V   Turns insert mode on/off.

^U   Deletes/undeletes a record.

^Q   Abandons, edits, and returns to dot prompt.

^W   Saves, edits, and returns to dot prompt.

To change the information of a field or record, just position the cursor where you want to make the change, and type the new data on top of the old data.

In the above example, the state and zip fields are not displayed because they can't fit on the screen with all the other information. To look at these fields, we need to pan to the right. Typing in a ^B will pan to the right one field, so the city would be displayed and the last name would be invisible. A second ^B would pan to the right another field, causing the zip to be displayed, but sending the first name off the screen.

When we are done browsing, we can use a ^W to save all data and return to the dot prompt.

Global Editing with CHANGE and REPLACE

In some cases we may wish to make the same change to numerous records in the data base. This is called *global editing*. For example, here in San Diego we recently had our area code changed from 714 to 619. Our MAIL data base doesn't have a field for phone numbers yet, so we can't try out this example. But if we had a data base with a field for phone numbers in it, we might want to scan through all the individuals who live in San Diego, and change their area codes. This could be accomplished by asking dBASE to

CHANGE FIELD PHONE FOR CITY = 'San Diego'   <RET>

The effect would be to display the phone number for each San Diego resident one at a time, so that we could change the area code. We tacked on the FOR CITY = 'San Diego' condition so that only the phone numbers for San Diego residents would be displayed. The resulting conversation might look something like this:

```
RECORD 00006
PHONE  : (714) 451-1212
CHANGE : 714
TO 619
PHONE  : (619) 451-1212
CHANGE?   <RET>

RECORD 00036
PHONE  : (714) 455-0101
CHANGE:714
TO 619
PHONE  : (619) 451-1212
CHANGE?   <RET>
```

etc.

dBASE will step through the data base, show us each San Diego resident's phone number, and allow us to change each one until we get to the end of the data base. This is a slow though safe means of performing a global edit. We can do things more quickly with the REPLACE command.

The REPLACE command is similar to the CHANGE command in that it changes the contents of a given field on a record. The REPLACE command, however, makes the change without asking questions. Here's a hypothetical example. Suppose that secretary A types in 500 names and addresses. She uses L.A. to stand for Los

Angeles in the CITY field. Secretary B comes in and adds 500 more names to the list, but she spells out Los Angeles rather than using the abbreviation. The dilemma? Anytime we want to do a mailing to Los Angeles, we have to do two: one for L.A. and one for Los Angeles. Lots of problems arise because our mindless computer has no idea that L.A. means Los Angeles. What's the solution? We could just change all the L.A.s to Los Angeles, or vice versa, but it would take a long time. This is where the REPLACE ALL command comes in handy. Observe how this command works:

        REPLACE ALL CITY WITH 'Los Angeles' FOR CITY = 'L.A.'
            <RET>

This one sentence says, "Anywhere you see L.A. as the city replace it with Los Angeles."

We must be very careful with this type of global editing, though, as the slightest mistake could ruin our data base. For example, *don't* type in the command to

        REPLACE ALL CITY WITH 'Los Angeles'   <RET>

or you will move everyone in the data base to Los Angeles. The hasty command above says, "Change *every* CITY field in *every* record to Los Angeles." Everyone in the data base would have Los Angeles as their city, whether their city was originally L.A., Cucamonga, or Seattle. The FOR CITY = 'L.A.' is necessary to make sure that only the L.A.s get changed.

We can try out the the REPLACE ALL command on our small MAIL data base just for fun. With MAIL in use, if we LIST the data base, we see

00001	Appleby	Andy	345 Oak St.	Los Angeles	CA	92123
00002	Smith	John Q.	123 A. St.	San Diego	CA	92123
00003	Smithsonian	Lucy	461 Adams St.	San Diego	CA	92122-1234
00004	Smith	Dave	123 B. St.	Los Angeles	CA	90123
00005	Doe	Ruth	1142 J. St.	Los Angeles	CA	91234
00006	SMITH	Betsy	222 Lemon Dr.	New York	NY	01234

Now let's type in the command to

> **REPLACE ALL STATE WITH 'HI' FOR STATE = 'CA'   < RET >**

dBASE informs us that it has performed

00005 REPLACEMENT(S)

Now if we do a LIST, we see that we just moved everyone in California to Hawaii.

00001	Appleby	Andy	345 Oak St.	Los Angeles	HI	92123
00002	Smith	John Q.	123 A. St.	San Diego	HI	92123
00003	Smithsonian	Lucy	461 Adams St.	San Diego	HI	92122-1234
00004	Smith	Dave	123 B. St.	Los Angeles	HI	90123
00005	Doe	Ruth	1142 J. St.	Los Angeles	HI	91234
00006	SMITH	Betsy	222 Lemon Dr.	New York	NY	01234

This could create a great deal of undeliverable mail for us, so we better reverse it. Simply type in the command to

> **REPLACE ALL STATE WITH 'CA' FOR STATE = 'HI'   < RET >**

and the MAIL data base will be back to its original form.

Like the LIST and DISPLAY commands, CHANGE and REPLACE can be used with any searching conditions to achieve a desired result. For example, the command

> **REPLACE ALL LNAME WITH 'Smith' FOR LNAME = 'SMITH'**

would change all the uppercase SMITHs to Smith. Likewise the command

> **CHANGE FIELD ZIP FOR ZIP < '10000'**

would step us through all the records with zip codes less than 10000 and allow us to change them. The possibilities are endless, and practice is the best teacher. With the REPLACE ALL command, however, it is best to practice on a backup data base rather than one that is important. The REPLACE ALL command has a high whoops factor.

By the time you get done saying "whoops," dBASE has already made the erroneous change to all records in the data base. Be careful.

Deleting from the Data Base
with DELETE, PACK, and RECALL

Sometimes we need to get rid of records in our data base. The DELETE command is used to mark records for deletion, and the PACK command is used to permanently delete records. Let's use Dave Smith as an example again. This time he does not renew his membership to our mailing list, so we want to eliminate him from our data base. First we need to find him on the data base. To do so, we

LIST FOR LNAME = 'Smith' .AND. FNAME = 'Dave'   <RET>

which gives us

00004   Smith   Dave   619 Elm St.   San Diego   CA   92122

We could ask dBASE to EDIT 4 (edit record 4), and then use a ^U to delete. A more direct approach would be to simply ask dBASE to

DELETE RECORD 4   <RET>

and dBASE informs us that it has performed

00001 DELETION(S)

Now, taking another look at our data base with a LIST, we see

00001	Appleby	Andy	345 Oak St.	Los Angeles	CA	92123
00002	Smith	John Q.	123 A. St.	San Diego	CA	92123
00003	Smithsonian	Lucy	461 Adams St.	San Diego	CA	92122-1234
00004 *	Smith	Dave	123 B. St.	Los Angeles	CA	90123
00005	Doe	Ruth	1142 J. St.	Los Angeles	CA	91234
00006	SMITH	Betsy	222 Lemon Dr.	New York	NY	01234

Dave is still there, but he is marked for deletion with an asterisk. Now we can say goodbye to Dave once and for all using this command:

PACK <RET>

dBASE replies

If we LIST our file now, we don't see Dave Smith.

00001	Appleby	Andy	345 Oak St.	Los Angeles	CA	92123
00002	Smith	John Q.	123 A. St.	San Diego	CA	92123
00003	Smithsonian	Lucy	461 Adams St.	San Diego	CA	92122-1234
00004	Doe	Ruth	1142 J. St.	Los Angeles	CA	91234
00005	SMITH	Betsy	222 Lemon Dr.	New York	NY	01234

Notice that everyone underneath Dave's original place in the data base has moved up a notch, and their record numbers have changed. We've packed in the empty spaces left open by deletions with active records. Remember, once you do a PACK, the record is gone forever. Prior to performing a PACK, however, we can reclaim records that are marked for deletion. For instance, let's

DELETE RECORD 2 <RET>

If we now LIST the data base, we see

00001	Appleby	Andy	345 Oak St.	Los Angeles	CA	92123
00002 *	Smith	John Q.	123 A. St.	San Diego	CA	92123
00003	Smithsonian	Lucy	461 Adams St.	San Diego	CA	92122-1234
00004	Doe	Ruth	1142 J. St.	Los Angeles	CA	91234
00005	SMITH	Betsy	222 Lemon Dr.	New York	NY	01234

Now John Q. Smith is marked for deletion. If we wish to call him back to the data base, we simply ask dBASE to

RECALL RECORD 2

Doing another LIST, we see

00001	Appleby	Andy	345 Oak St.	Los Angeles	CA	92123
00002	Smith	John Q.	123 A. St.	San Diego	CA	92123
00003	Smithsonian	Lucy	461 Adams St.	San Diego	CA	92122-1234
00004	Doe	Ruth	1142 J. St.	Los Angeles	CA	91234
00005	SMITH	Betsy	222 Lemon Dr.	New York	NY	01234

John Q. Smith is no longer marked for deletion, so a PACK procedure would not eliminate him from our data base.

We can also perform global deletions, using the command to DELETE ALL FOR (some condition). If we wanted to do a quick job of deleting all the people in California from our data base, we could simply type in the command to

DELETE ALL FOR STATE = 'CA' <RET>

dBASE would respond with

00004 DELETION(S)

The effect of this command would be to mark all records with CA in the state field for deletion. If we were to list the contents of the data base now, we'd see

00001 *	Appleby	Andy	345 Oak St.	Los Angeles	CA	92123
00002 *	Smith	John Q.	123 A. St.	San Diego	CA	92123
00003 *	Smithsonian	Lucy	461 Adams St.	San Diego	CA	92122-1234
00004 *	Doe	Ruth	1142 J. St.	Los Angeles	CA	91234
00005	SMITH	Betsy	222 Lemon Dr.	New York	NY	01234

All individuals who live in California are marked for deletion. Don't PACK them now, or we'll end up with only one record in our data base, Betsy SMITH, since she lives in New York. Rather than packing, let's

RECALL ALL <RET>

so that we don't lose all our California residents permanently. (The big earthquake hasn't hit yet, but the practice might be useful.) If we LIST after recalling all the records we'll see

00001	Appleby	Andy	345 Oak St.	Los Angeles	CA	92123
00002	Smith	John Q.	123 A. St.	San Diego	CA	92123
00003	Smithsonian	Lucy	461 Adams St.	San Diego	CA	92122-1234
00004	Doe	Ruth	1142 J. St.	Los Angeles	CA	91234
00005	SMITH	Betsy	222 Lemon Dr.	New York	NY	01234

Everyone is back in shape.

Global deletes are useful for getting the job done quickly, but there is an element of danger: we might accidentally delete records we wanted to keep. It's a good idea always to LIST the records that are marked for deletion prior to packing the data base. For example, suppose we decided to take a shortcut method for deleting John Smith from the data base using the command

    DELETE ALL FOR LNAME = 'Smith'   **<RET>**

We would end up with the response

    00002 DELETION(S)

Whoops. We had actually only planned to delete one Smith, but ended up with two deletions. So to see who else we've accidentally deleted, we would ask dBASE to

    LIST FOR *   **<RET>**

That is, list all the records that are marked for deletion. The result would be

00002 *	Smith	John Q.	123 A. St.	San Diego	CA	92123
00003 *	Smithsonian	Lucy	462 Adams St.	San Diego	CA	92122-1234

Apparently we've gotten a little carried away with our global delete here. We only meant to delete John Q. Smith, but, unfortunately our global delete marked Lucy Smithsonian for deletion also. We can bring back Lucy with the command to

RECALL RECORD 3   < RET >

dBASE would release record 3 from deletion. Global deletes are useful in cases where we want to delete records of a certain type, but be sure to LIST FOR * prior to PACKing to make sure you won't be deleting any innocents. Now type in the command

RECALL ALL   < RET >

so that we don't lose John Q. Smith permanently.

The DELETE command can also be used to delete an entire data base. Remember when we were using the SORT command, we would SORT TO B:TEMP. That means old B:TEMP.DBF is still taking up space on the disk. We can get rid of TEMP right now by typing in the command

DELETE FILE B:TEMP.DBF   < RET >

dBASE will respond with the comment

FILE HAS BEEN DELETED

Once you delete an entire file, you can't get it back without extra help. So do be careful. If you should ever accidentally delete a whole data base that was important to you, there are several software packages on the market that might bring them back to life. "Disk Doctor" by Super Soft is one such product. If you ever realize that you've accidentally deleted an important file, do not put anything else on that disk prior to attempting to reclaim it with the appropriate software, or it will be too late.

MODIFY STRUCTURE of a Data Base

The issue of adding telephone numbers to our data base has popped up a couple of times. Let's take care of that now by modifying the structure of our data base to include a field for phone numbers. The command for this is MODIFY STRUCTURE. *Important note:* you must *always* make a copy of your original data base first, as the MODIFY STRUCTURE eliminates *all* data in a data base. Let's get started. Type in the commands to

    USE B:MAIL   <RET>
    COPY TO B:TEMP   <RET>

These two commands name MAIL as the file in use, then make a copy of MAIL's contents to a file called TEMP. Now let's

    MODIFY STRUCTURE   <RET>

dBASE has a built-in warning to give us a chance to change our minds, just in case we forgot to make a backup copy of the data base. You will now see

MODIFY ERASES ALL RECORDS IN A DATA BASE. PROCEED? (Y/N) :

I always feel a little queasy answering yes to this question, but since we have safely copied the MAIL data base to a data base called TEMP, our data will not be lost. Once we answer affirmatively, we see

	NAME	TYP	LEN	DEC
FIELD 01	:LNAME	C	020	000
FIELD 02	:FNAME	C	010	000
FIELD 03	:ADDRESS	C	020	000
FIELD 04	:CITY	C	010	000
FIELD 05	:STATE	C	005	000
FIELD 06	:ZIP	C	010	000
FIELD 07	:			
FIELD 08	:			

We can see the cursor ready under LNAME. Now, pop quiz. What type of data will the phone number be, character or numeric? If you guessed numeric, then you indeed just guessed. Perhaps the word "number" in "phone number" threw you off. What might a typical phone number look like? Perhaps 453-0121, or (619) 555-1212, or maybe there are two: W:555-1212 and H:555-1313. There are lots of nonnumeric characters floating around these numbers, especially the infamous hyphen sign, which means "subtract" in computer talk. A phone number is a character type. Its width? Well, let's take a liberal case: W:(619) 453-7120 H:(619) 455-1212. That one is 35 characters wide, so we'll make our PHONE field 35 characters wide.

Field 7 seems as good as any for putting in the phone number, so we can just move the cursor down to that field in the usual fashion (control-key command ^X). When we get there, type in

    PHONE   C   035   000   <RET>

so that the screen display looks like this:

FIELD 01	:LNAME	C	020	000
FIELD 02	:FNAME	C	010	000
FIELD 03	:ADDRESS	C	020	000
FIELD 04	:CITY	C	010	000
FIELD 05	:STATE	C	005	000
FIELD 06	:ZIP	C	010	000
FIELD 07	:PHONE	C	035	000
FIELD 08	:_			
FIELD 09	:			

Next, a ^W will save the new structure and send us back to the dot prompt. If we now do a LIST, we get

.

nothing. dBASE wasn't kidding about erasing all the records. We've got our names and addresses stored in TEMP though, so now we can

    APPEND FROM B:TEMP   <RET>

which gives us the message 5 RECORDS ADDED and the dot prompt. If we do a LIST now, we will see that all of our records are intact. Of course, there are no phone numbers yet. And I'm afraid that there is no dBASE command to automatically fill in the phone numbers for us. We need to put those in using the EDIT command. If we ask dBASE to EDIT 2 (edit record 2) we'll see

```
RECORD 00002
LNAME     :Smith          :
FNAME     :John Q.     :
ADDRESS :123 A. St.             :
CITY      :San Diego      :
STATE     :CA   :
ZIP       :92123      :
PHONE   :                          :
```

Notice that there is now a new field at the bottom of the EDIT display in which to put phone numbers. We can move the cursor down five lines by typing in five ^Xs, so that the cursor would be in the PHONE field, like so:

```
PHONE:_                          :
```

Then we can type in the phone number:

```
PHONE:(555) 453-1212_                 :
```

and save the new data with a ^W. The APPEND command would permit phone numbers too. So in this last example, we've modified the structure of the data base, and created a new field so that we can add phone numbers to each record.

NOTE: You've probably noticed by now that whenever you fill up any field in an EDIT screen format (as well as any APPEND screen format), the computer beeps and the cursor jumps down to the next field in the display. If you find this bell irritating, you can get rid of it by changing a basic dBASE parameter. The command

```
    SET BELL OFF   <RET>
```

typed in next to the dBASE dot prompt will keep the bell from beeping or ringing when you fill up one of the fields on the EDIT or APPEND screens.

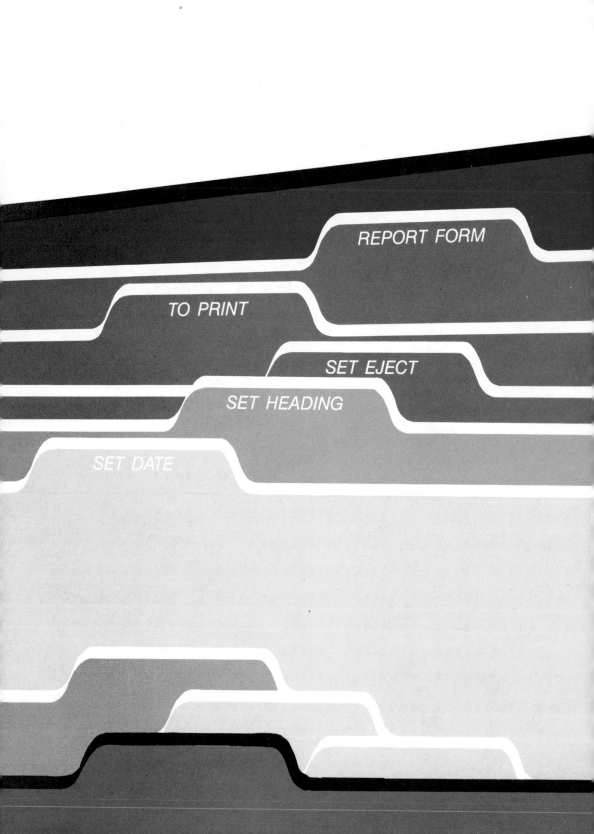

REPORT FORM

TO PRINT

SET EJECT

SET HEADING

SET DATE

CREATING AND PRINTING FORMATTED REPORTS

6

So far we've been displaying our data on the screen without any particular format. I've even cheated a little in displaying LISTs in this book so that they would fit the page. If we don't provide dBASE with an exact format for displaying our data, dBASE will list records and fields in its own fashion. To print formatted reports with dBASE II, we use its built-in report generator.

REPORT FORM

The procedure for creating report formats is simple. Whenever we create a report format, we need to give it a file name so that dBASE can easily find it later. The names used for report forms can be up to eight characters in length. Remember that spaces and punctuation marks should not be used. dBASE stores the report format on a data file and adds the last name .FRM. So if we create a report format called BYNAME, dBASE will store this format in a file called BYNAME.FRM. Let's create a report format now for our MAIL file that displays the records on our data base in a directory fashion. First we need to get dBASE up and running. Then we need to

USE B:MAIL   <RET>

Now let's ask dBASE to set up a report form on the file named BYNAME. Type in

REPORT FORM B:BYNAME   <RET>

dBASE will first check to see if BYNAME.FRM already exists on the disk in drive B. If not, it will ask for the format on the screen in the following fashion:

ENTER OPTIONS, M = LEFT MARGIN, L = LINES/PAGE,
    W = PAGE WIDTH

Now we have a chance to be creative. Let's put the left margin all the way to the left (column 1). If we use an 80-column printer, we'll set the right margin to 80. To do so, we must type

M = 1, W = 80   <RET>

which brings up the question

PAGE HEADING (Y/N) ?

We do want to have the heading printed at the top of the page, so we type Y. Next dBASE asks us to

ENTER PAGE HEADING:

to which we reply MAILING LIST BY NAME < RET >. Then dBASE wants to know if it should

DOUBLE SPACE REPORT? (Y/N)

No thanks, single space is fine. We'll type in N. Next dBASE asks

ARE TOTALS REQUIRED? (Y/N)

No. Since we are not doing math, this won't be necessary. Now dBASE wants the column formats.

COL   WIDTH,CONTENTS
001 _

   We'll put the last name in the first column, and make it 15 spaces wide. So we type in

   15,LNAME   < RET >

and dBASE asks us to

ENTER HEADING:

We'll type in Last Name and press < RET >. Then, we repeat the same sequence for column two, column three, and so forth. Here is everything we entered for our report:

ENTER OPTIONS, M = LEFT MARGIN,L = LINES/PAGE,
   W = PAGE WIDTH M = 1,W = 80
PAGE HEADING? (Y/N) Y
ENTER PAGE HEADING: MAILING LIST BY NAME
DOUBLE SPACE REPORT? (Y/N) N
ARE TOTALS REQUIRED? (Y/N) N
COL WIDTH,CONTENTS
001 15,LNAME
ENTER HEADING:Last Name
002 10,FNAME

ENTER HEADING:First Name

003   15,ADDRESS

ENTER HEADING:Address

004 13,CITY

ENTER HEADING:City

005 5,STATE

ENTER HEADING:State

006 10,ZIP

ENTER HEADING:Zip code

007   <RET>

We have set up a format for a report with six columns in it, each one holding an individual field. By pressing the RETURN key when dBASE asked for the seventh column, the report generation was put into effect. So in a couple of seconds we should see

PAGE NO. 00001

MAILING LIST BY NAMES

Last name	First Name	Address	City	State	Zip
Appleby	Andy	345 Oak St.	Los Angeles	CA	92123
Smith	John Q.	123 A. St.	San Diego	CA	92123
Smithsonian	Lucy	461 Adams St.	San Diego	CA	92122-1234
Doe	Ruth	1142 J. St.	Los Angeles	CA	91234
SMITH	Betsy	222 Lemon Dr.	New York	NY	01234

We have a neater format than the one generated by the LIST command. By the way, you've probably noticed that when you first boot up dBASE, it asks for the date. If you fill in the date there, the date will appear under the page number on the report.

One disadvantage to our nicely formatted report is that it is not sorted. We can easily rectify this by INDEXing the data base into our desired order before printing it. If we wish to format our report in alphabetical order, we type in

INDEX ON LNAME TO B:NAMES   <RET>

When the index is complete, we

REPORT FORM B:BYNAME   <RET>

and get

PAGE NO. 00001

                    MAILING LIST BY NAMES

Last name	First Name	Address	City	State	Zip
Appleby	Andy	345 Oak St.	Los Angeles	CA	92123
Doe	Ruth	1142 J. St.	Los Angeles	CA	91234
SMITH	Betsy	222 Lemon Dr.	New York	NY	01234
Smith	John Q.	123 A. St.	San Diego	CA	92123
Smithsonian	Lucy	461 Adams St.	San Diego	CA	92122-1234

This time the report was printed in proper order immediately, without requiring us to redefine the format. This is because when we asked dBASE to

REPORT FORM B:BYNAME

it found that a file called BYNAME.FRM already existed on the disk in drive B, so it just used that existing report format.

Let's try a little fancier report, one listed by zip code. First, we will get the zip code order:

USE B:MAIL   <RET>
INDEX ON ZIP + LNAME + FNAME TO B:FANCY   <RET>

Now we'll set up a report form called BYZIP on drive B:

REPORT FORM B:BYZIP   <RET>

and fill in the blanks like so:

ENTER OPTIONS, M = LEFT MARGIN,L = LINES/PAGE,
    W = PAGE WIDTH M = 1,W = 80
PAGE HEADING? (Y/N) Y
ENTER PAGE HEADING: MAILING LIST;SORTED BY
    ZIP CODE AND NAME
DOUBLE SPACE REPORT? (Y/N) N

```
ARE TOTALS REQUIRED? (Y/N) N
COL WIDTH,CONTENTS
001 15,ZIP
ENTER HEADING:Zip Code
002 30,TRIM(LNAME)+', '+FNAME
ENTER HEADING:Name
003 15,ADDRESS
ENTER HEADING:Address
004 13,CITY
ENTER HEADING:City
005 5,STATE
ENTER HEADING:State
006    <RET>
```

We get this report:

PAGE 00001

MAILING LIST
SORTED BY ZIP CODE AND NAME

Zip Code	Name	Address	City	State
01234	SMITH, Betsy	222 Lemon Dr.	New York	NY
91234	Doe, Ruth	1142 J. St.	Los Angeles	CA
92122-1234	Smithsonian, Lucy	461 Adams St.	San Diego	CA
92123	Appleby, Andy	345 Oak St.	Los Angeles	CA
92123	Smith, John Q.	123 A. St.	San Diego	CA

Notice that the title is centered on two lines. This was accomplished with a semicolon (;) by entering the heading as MAILING LIST;SORTED BY ZIP CODE AND NAME. Also notice that the first and last names are closer together. We did this by placing TRIM(LNAME)+', '+ FNAME in the second column. This says, "Print the last name with trailing blanks removed, followed by a comma and a space, followed by the first name." It looks nicer, don't you think? If you have a printer hooked up, you can print the report by simply asking dBASE to

REPORT FORM B:BYZIP TO PRINT   <RET>

Of course, we might want to include only a specific zip code batch or city in the report. If so, we can use the FOR command with the REPORT command to narrow down the items in the report. For example, the command

    REPORT FORM B:BYZIP FOR ZIP = '92123'   <RET>

asks dBASE to include only those individuals in the 92123 zip code area. The command to

    REPORT FORM B:BYZIP FOR CITY = 'San Diego';
        TO PRINT   <RET>

asks dBASE to include only San Diego residents in the report, and sends the report to the printer.

Report Format Parameters

There are several general dBASE parameters that we can use to alter our reports. The PLAIN parameter can be used to leave the page number off of a report. For example, if we type in the command

    REPORT FORM B:BYZIP PLAIN   <RET>

the BYZIP report in this case will be printed according to the format designated in the BYZIP.FRM file, but the page number will be left off of the report. If we now want the date to appear on the report, even though we did not enter one when we first loaded up dBASE, we can still

    SET DATE TO 04/30/83   <RET>

and that date will appear directly beneath the page number when we ask dBASE to REPORT FORM BYZIP. This date *must* use two digits each for month/day/year (MM/DD/YY) for dBASE to accept it as valid. If we want our report to display the date in a more formal manner (e.g. June 11, 1983), we can have it displayed above the heading of the report. But first, to make sure that the dBASE date (06/11/83) doesn't appear also, we should

    SET DATE TO 0   <RET>

Then type in the command to

> SET HEADING TO June 11, 1983   < RET >

Then when the dot prompt reappears, go ahead and REPORT FORM B:BYZIP. The report will come out looking like this:

PAGE 00001   June 11, 1983
                         MAILING LIST
                SORTED BY ZIP CODE AND NAME

Zip Code	Name	Address	City	State
01234	SMITH, Betsy	222 Lemon Dr.	New York	NY
91234	Doe, Ruth	1142 J. St.	Los Angeles	CA
92122-1234	Smithsonian, Lucy	461 Adams St.	San Diego	CA
92123	Appleby, Andy	345 Oak St.	Los Angeles	CA
92123	Smith, John Q.	123 A. St.	San Diego	CA

You may have also noticed that if you send a report to the printer, the paper first advances to a new page. If you do not wish this to occur, you can ask dBASE to

> SET EJECT OFF   < RET >

and this will prevent the initial form feed before the report is sent to the printer.

The REPORT FORM also allows us to include totals and subtotals in our report, but since our MAIL data base has no numeric fields we can't experiment with these just yet. In the next chapter, we'll create a new data base with numbers, which will allow us to further explore the REPORT FORM command.

In Appendix A we discuss methods in which you can send dBASE reports to your word processing system, using the WordStar package as the example. This is very handy for embedding dBASE reports inside of WordStar documents. It also allows you to modify your dBASE reports to any format you like.

MANAGING NUMBERS IN A DATA BASE

7

dBASE II has several capabilites for doing basic arithmetic in data bases. Our MAIL data base did not require such manipulations, so in this chapter we'll create a new data base and try out some new commands. We'll discuss the totalling and subtotalling capabilities of the REPORT FORM command, and also experiment with SUM, COUNT, and ?.

Managing Numeric Data

To learn techniques for managing numbers we'll create a new data base called SALES. It will have fields for product code, product description, quantity sold, amount of sale, and date of sale. To create this data base we need to have the dBASE dot prompt ready on our screen, then we

    CREATE B:SALES <RET>

We've selected drive B once again for storing the data. As usual, dBASE gives us a form to fill in describing the structure of the data base. Here's how the form should look on the screen after we've filled in all the information:

ENTER RECORD STRUCTURE AS FOLLOWS:

FIELD	NAME,TYPE,WIDTH,DECIMAL PLACES
001	CODE,C,5
002	TITLE,C,15
003	QTY,N,5,0
004	AMOUNT,N,12,2
005	DATE,C,9
006	—

Notice that CODE, TITLE, and DATE are all character (C) types. QTY (quantity) is a numeric (N) type with a maximum width of five and no decimal places. AMOUNT is also numeric, with a maximum of twelve digits, including two digits for decimal places. Two decimal places are necessary because this is a dollar amount. When we get to the sixth field, we press RETURN and dBASE asks

INPUT DATA NOW?

If you are ready to type in the data below, answer Y. Otherwise, you can answer N and APPEND the data later. Here are the data we will be using for our examples. Let's type these in.

CODE	TITLE	QTY	AMOUNT	DATE
AAA	Rakes	3	15.00	03/01/83
BBB	Hoes	2	12.50	03/01/83
CCC	Shovels	3	21.00	03/01/83
AAA	Rakes	2	10.00	03/01/83
CCC	Shovels	4	26.50	03/01/83
AAA	Rakes	2	11.00	03/02/83
CCC	Shovels	1	7.50	03/02/83
BBB	Hoes	2	12.50	03/02/83
AAA	Rakes	5	23.50	03/02/83

When dBASE asks for the tenth record, just press RETURN so that the dot prompt appears.

SUM and COUNT

Now we can experiment with some new commands. Suppose we wanted to know how much our gross sales were. We would need to sum the amounts using the command

SUM AMOUNT   <RET>

dBASE replies with

139.50

We might want to know both the quantity of items sold and the total sales. The command to find out is

SUM QTY,AMOUNT   <RET>

to which dBASE replies

24 139.50

We may want to sum data for specific records only. For example, suppose we want to know how product AAA, rakes, is selling. We could ask dBASE to

    SUM QTY,AMOUNT FOR CODE = 'AAA' <RET>

dBASE sums the quantities and amounts for product code AAA, and displays the answer as

12 59.50

To get a quick look at the unit price for this product, we can ask dBASE for the quotient of 59.50 divided by 12 (the sales dollars divided by quantity sold). The command to do so is

    ? 59.50/12

dBASE replies with

4.95

Therefore, the average unit price for product code AAA is $4.95. If we wanted to know how much we sold on a certain date, we could ask dBASE to

    SUM AMOUNT FOR DATE = '03/01/83' <RET>

dBASE informs us that on March 1, we sold

85.00

dollars worth of materials. Being even more specific, we might want dBASE to tell us how much of product AAA we sold on March 1. The command to find this out is

    SUM AMOUNT FOR CODE = 'AAA' .AND.
        DATE = '03/01/83' <RET>

to which dBASE replies with

25.00

   In some cases we might prefer to know how many records contain certain information, rather than knowing about sums of fields. For example, we might wish to know how many transactions took place on a given date (assuming one record equals one transaction). We use the COUNT command for this. To find out how many records on the data base have 03/01/83 as the date, we would ask dBASE to

COUNT FOR DATE = '03/01/83'   <RET>

dBASE will tell us that

COUNT = 00005

There are five records dated 03/01/83. To see how many transactions took place on March 1 for product code AAA, we'd type in the command

COUNT FOR DATE = '03/01/83' .AND. CODE = 'AAA'   <RET>

dBASE would tell us that

COUNT = 00002

That is, there are two records on the data base that have 03/01/83 as the date and AAA as the product code.

In short, the SUM command adds up numeric fields, and the COUNT command counts how many records in the data base have some particular characteristic. The SUM FOR and COUNT FOR commands can use all the searching conditions that the LIST FOR command can use, so we can be pretty specific about our sums and countings.

Total and Subtotal in Reports

When our data base has numeric fields in it, we can use the REPORT FORM's capabilities to generate totals and subtotals in our reports. Whether or not our report has totals or subtotals depends upon how we answer the questions that the REPORT FORM command brings up. Let's try some examples.

We can get a pretty straightforward report with totals for quantity and amount by asking dBASE to

REPORT FORM B:TOTALS   <RET>

and answering its questions as follows:

```
ENTER OPTIONS, M=LEFT MARGIN,L=LINES/PAGE,
    W=PAGE WIDTH   <RET>
PAGE HEADING? (Y/N) Y
ENTER PAGE HEADING Total Sales
DOUBLE SPACE REPORT? (Y/N) N
ARE TOTALS REQUIRED? (Y/N) Y
SUBTOTALS IN REPORT? (Y/N) N
COL   WIDTH,CONTENTS
001    5,CODE
ENTER HEADING: Code
002    15,TITLE
ENTER HEADING: Title
003    5,QTY
ENTER HEADING: Qty
ARE TOTALS REQUIRED? (Y/N) Y
004    12,AMOUNT
ENTER HEADING: Amount
ARE TOTALS REQUIRED? (Y/N) Y
005    8,DATE
ENTER HEADING: Date
006    <RET>
```

As soon as we're done entering the format, dBASE prints the following report:

```
PAGE NO. 00001

                       Total Sales

Code          Title           Qty          Amount          Date
AAA           Rakes           3            15.00           03/01/83
BBB           Hoes            2            12.50           03/01/83
CCC           Shovels         3            21.00           03/01/83
AAA           Rakes           2            10.00           03/01/83
CCC           Shovels         4            26.50           03/01/83
```

AAA	Rakes	2	11.00	03/02/83
CCC	Shovels	1	7.50	03/02/83
BBB	Hoes	2	12.50	03/02/83
AAA	Rakes	5	23.50	03/02/83

* * TOTAL * *

		24	139.50	

Here we get a formatted report with totals for quantity and amount displayed. We may prefer to have sales subtotalled by product code. To do so, we must first SORT or INDEX our data base by this field. Using the INDEX command, we would

INDEX ON CODE TO B:CODES   < RET>

Then we would create a report format that included subtotals. To do so, we would

REPORT FORM B:BYCODE   < RET>

and fill out the format questionnaire as follows:

```
ENTER OPTIONS, M = LEFT MARGIN,L = LINES/PAGE,
     W = PAGE WIDTH   <RET>
PAGE HEADING? (Y/N) Y
ENTER PAGE HEADING Sales by Product Code
DOUBLE SPACE REPORT? (Y/N) N
ARE TOTALS REQUIRED? (Y/N) Y
SUBTOTALS IN REPORT? (Y/N) Y
ENTER SUBTOTALS FIELD: CODE
SUMMARY REPORT ONLY? (Y/N) N
EJECT PAGE AFTER SUBTOTALS? (Y/N) N
ENTER SUBTOTAL HEADING: Product Code
COL   WIDTH,CONTENTS
001    5,CODE
ENTER HEADING: Code
002    15,TITLE
ENTER HEADING: Title
003    5,QTY
ENTER HEADING: Qty
```

ARE TOTALS REQUIRED? (Y/N) Y
004   12,AMOUNT
ENTER HEADING: Amount
ARE TOTALS REQUIRED? (Y/N) Y
005   8,DATE
ENTER HEADING: Date
006   <RET>

dBASE will then generate the following report:

PAGE NO. 00001

Sales by Product Code

Code	Title	Qty	Amount	Date
* Product Code AAA				
AAA	Rakes	3	15.00	03/01/83
AAA	Rakes	2	10.00	03/01/83
AAA	Rakes	2	11.00	03/02/83
AAA	Rakes	5	23.50	03/02/83
* * SUBTOTAL * *				
		12	59.50	
* Product Code BBB				
BBB	Hoes	2	12.50	03/01/83
BBB	Hoes	2	12.50	03/02/83
* * SUBTOTAL * *				
		4	25.00	
* Product Code CCC				
CCC	Shovels	3	21.00	03/01/83
CCC	Shovels	4	26.50	03/01/83
CCC	Shovels	1	7.50	03/02/83
* * SUBTOTAL * *				
		8	55.00	
* * TOTAL * *				
		24	139.50	

This report gives us a breakdown of sales by product code. Should we want to subtotal by the sales of each day, we would need to INDEX ON DATE TO B:DATE first, then create a REPORT FORM B:BYDATE, and tell dBASE to subtotal on DATE when it asked us to ENTER SUBTOTALS FIELD.

In some cases, we might wish to subtotal on more than one field. For example, suppose we wanted our report to subtotal by both date and product code so that we could see how each product sold on each date. First, we would need to index on these two fields using the command

INDEX ON DATE + CODE TO B:DATECODE   <RET>

Then we would ask dBASE to

REPORT FORM B:DATECODE   <RET>

Next we would need to fill out the form as follows:

```
ENTER OPTIONS, M=LEFT MARGIN,L=LINES/PAGE,
    W=PAGE WIDTH    <RET>
PAGE HEADING? (Y/N) Y
ENTER PAGE HEADING Sales by Date and Product Code
DOUBLE SPACE REPORT? (Y/N) N
ARE TOTALS REQUIRED? (Y/N) Y
SUBTOTALS IN REPORT? (Y/N) Y
ENTER SUBTOTALS FIELD: DATE+CODE
SUMMARY REPORT ONLY? (Y/N) N
EJECT PAGE AFTER SUBTOTALS? (Y/N) N
ENTER SUBTOTAL HEADING: Date and Code:
COL    WIDTH,CONTENTS
001    8,DATE
ENTER HEADING: Date
002    6,CODE
ENTER HEADING: Code
003    15,TITLE
ENTER HEADING: Title
004    6,QTY
```

ARE TOTALS REQUIRED? (Y/N) Y
ENTER HEADING: Qty
005   12,AMOUNT
ENTER HEADING: Amount
ARE TOTALS REQUIRED? (Y/N) Y
006   < RET>

dBASE will then generate the following report:

PAGE NO. 00001

Sales by Date and Product Code

Date	Code	Title	Qty	Amount
* Date and Code 03/01/83 AAA				
03/01/83	AAA	Rakes	3	15.00
03/01/83	AAA	Rakes	2	10.00
* * SUBTOTAL * *				
			5	25.00
* Date and Code 03/01/83 BBB				
03/01/83	BBB	Hoes	2	12.50
* * SUBTOTAL * *				
			2	12.50
* Date and Code 03/01/83 CCC				
03/01/83	CCC	Shovels	3	21.00
03/01/83	CCC	Shovels	4	26.50
* * SUBTOTAL * *				
			7	47.50
* Date and Code 03/02/83 AAA				
03/02/83	AAA	Rakes	2	11.00
03/02/83	AAA	Rakes	5	23.50
* * SUBTOTAL * *				
			7	34.50
* Date and Code 03/02/83 BBB				
03/02/83	BBB	Hoes	2	12.50
* * SUBTOTAL * *				
			2	12.50

```
*  Date and Code 03/02/83 CCC
03/02/83          CCC          Shovels          1              7.50
* * SUBTOTAL * *
                                                 1              7.50

* * TOTAL * *
                                                24            139.50
```

Notice that for each day, the quantities and amounts are sub-totalled by product code, just as we requested.

dBASE can also provide us with summary reports of our data. Let's create a report form called SUMMARY, just like the DATECODE form, but this time we'll answer Y to the SUMMARY REPORT ONLY? question. We'll also change the report heading. Let's type in

REPORT FORM B:SUMMARY   <RET>

and answer the questions as follows:

```
ENTER OPTIONS, M = LEFT MARGIN, L = LINES/PAGE,
    W = PAGE WIDTH; M = 1,W = 50
PAGE HEADING? (Y/N) Y
ENTER PAGE HEADING: Summary of Sales;By Date and Product Code
DOUBLE SPACE REPORT? (Y/N) N
ARE TOTALS REQUIRED? (Y/N) Y
SUBTOTALS IN REPORT? (Y/N) Y
ENTER SUBTOTALS FIELD: DATE + CODE
SUMMARY REPORT ONLY? (Y/N) Y
EJECT PAGE AFTER SUBTOTALS? (Y/N) N
ENTER SUBTOTAL HEADING: Date and Code:
COL    WIDTH,CONTENTS
001    9,DATE
ENTER HEADING: Date
002    5,CODE
ENTER HEADING: Code
003    15,TITLE
ENTER HEADING: Title
004    5,Qty
```

```
ENTER HEADING: Qty
ARE TOTALS REQUIRED? (Y/N) Y
005    12,Amount
ENTER HEADING: Amount
ARE TOTALS REQUIRED? (Y/N) Y
006    <RET>
```

dBASE generates the following report:

PAGE NO. 00001

Summary of Sales

By Date and Product Code

Date	Code	Title	Qty	Amount
* Date and Code: 03/01/83 AAA				
* * SUBTOTAL * *				
			5	25.00
* Date and Code: 03/01/83 BBB				
* * SUBTOTAL * *				
			2	12.50
* Date and Code: 03/01/83 CCC				
* * SUBTOTAL * *				
			7	47.50
* Date and Code: 03/02/83 AAA				
* * SUBTOTAL * *				
			7	34.50
* Date and Code: 03/02/83 BBB				
* * SUBTOTAL * *				
			2	12.50
* Date and Code: 03/02/83 CCC				
* * SUBTOTAL * *				
			1	7.50
* * TOTAL * *				
			24	139.50

In this report, only the subtotalled data are displayed. The individual transactions are left out.

Performing Calculations in Report Columns

We can do arithmetic in our report columns also. Suppose we wanted to know the unit price for each transaction. The unit price is the amount divided by the quantity. We could simply place a field in the formatted report which prints AMOUNT/QTY. In the following report, named UNITS, we provide this capability. Furthermore, we're going to subtotal by date and product code. We've already created an index for date by product code order, so let's first

    USE B:SALES INDEX B:DATECODE   < RET >

Then we'll

    REPORT FORM B:UNITS   < RET >

and fill out the format questionnaire as follows:

```
ENTER OPTIONS, M = LEFT MARGIN, L = LINES/PAGE,
    W = PAGE WIDTH    < RET >
PAGE HEADING? (Y/N) Y
ENTER PAGE HEADING: Sales by Date and Code;With Unit Price
DOUBLE SPACE REPORT? (Y/N) N
ARE TOTALS REQUIRED? (Y/N) Y
SUBTOTALS IN REPORT? (Y/N) Y
ENTER SUBTOTALS FIELD: DATE + CODE
SUMMARY REPORT ONLY? (Y/N) N
EJECT PAGE AFTER SUBTOTALS? (Y/N) N
ENTER SUBTOTAL HEADING: Date and Code:
COL    WIDTH,CONTENTS
001    10,DATE
ENTER HEADING: Date
002    6,CODE
ENTER HEADING: Code
003    12,TITLE
ENTER HEADING: Title
004    6,QTY
```

ENTER HEADING: Qty

ARE TOTALS REQUIRED? (Y/N) Y

005   12,AMOUNT

ENTER HEADING: Amount

ARE TOTALS REQUIRED? (Y/N) Y

006   12,AMOUNT/QTY

ENTER HEADING: Unit Price

ARE TOTALS REQUIRED? (Y/N) N

007

dBASE then generates the following report:

PAGE NO. 00001

Sales by Date and Code
With Unit Price

Date	Code	Title	Qty	Amount	Unit Price
* Date and Code: 03/01/83 AAA					
03/01/83	AAA	Rakes	3	15.00	5.00
03/01/83	AAA	Rakes	2	10.00	5.00
* * SUBTOTAL * *					
			5	25.00	10.00
* Date and Code: 03/01/83 BBB					
03/01/83	BBB	Hoes	2	12.50	6.25
* * SUBTOTAL * *					
			2	12.50	6.25
* Date and Code: 03/01/83 CCC					
03/01/83	CCC	Shovels	3	21.00	7.00
03/01/83	CCC	Shovels	4	26.50	6.62
* * SUBTOTAL * *					
			7	47.50	13.62
* Date and Code: 03/02/83 AAA					
03/02/83	AAA	Rakes	2	11.00	5.50
03/02/83	AAA	Rakes	5	23.50	4.70
* * SUBTOTAL * *					
			7	34.50	10.20

```
*  Date and Code: 03/02/83 BBB
03/02/83        BBB         Hoes            2           12.50           6.25
* * SUBTOTAL * *
                                            2           12.50           6.25
*  Date and Code: 03/02/83 CCC
03/02/83        CCC         Shovels         1            7.50           7.50
* * SUBTOTAL * *
                                            1            7.50           7.50
* * TOTAL          * *
                                           24          139.50
```

This report gives us the unit price for each transaction. That is, we see in the first row that three rakes were sold for $15.00, so the unit price is $5.00. On March 2, two rakes were sold for $11.00, so the unit price is $5.50. Bear in mind that the data base itself has no field for unit price, yet the report has a column entitled "Unit Price." This was accomplished by making the sixth column of the report contain AMOUNT/QTY (amount divided by quantity).

You are probably starting to realize how useful dBASE II can be in organizing and arranging data to your specifications. So far we've only scratched the surface of the potential power of dBASE II. In the next chapters, we'll discuss how to manage multiple data files.

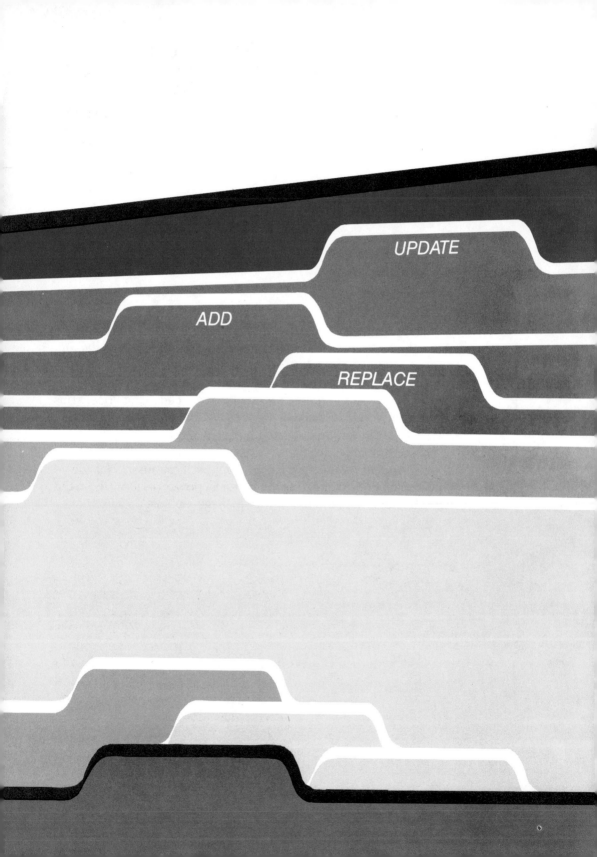

MANAGING MULTIPLE DATA FILES

8

In the last chapter, we created a data base called SALES to keep track of business sales figures. Most businesses also need to keep a record of goods received and overall inventory too. To allow dBASE to manage this much data, we need to develop three separate data bases: one for sales, one for new stock, and a master inventory data base. We can envision the relationship among the three data bases in Figure 8.1.

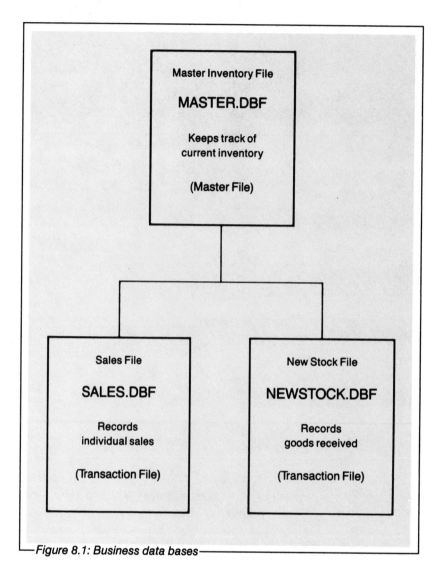

Figure 8.1: Business data bases

We refer to the sales and new stock files as transaction files, because they contain information about individual transactions involved in buying and selling goods. The inventory file is the master file, because it represents the status of the inventory, based upon information from the two transaction files. We must occasionally update the master file from the transaction files, and that is what this chapter explains.

An Inventory System

First, let's create the master inventory file, and give it the filename MASTER.

CREATE B:MASTER   <RET>

Let's give it the following structure:

```
ENTER RECORD STRUCTURE AS FOLLOWS:
FIELD    NAME,TYPE,WIDTH,DECIMAL PLACES
00001    CODE,C,5
00002    TITLE,C,15
00003    QTY,N,5,0
00004    PRICE,N,12,2
00005    REORDER,N,5,0
00006
```

When dBASE asks if we want to INPUT DATA NOW? (Y/N), we'll answer Y and type in the following data:

CODE	TITLE	QTY	PRICE	REORDER
1) AAA	Rakes	30	3.50	25
2) BBB	Hoes	30	4.50	25
3) CCC	Shovels	30	5.00	25

When we're done typing in the data, we can

USE B:MASTER   <RET>
LIST   <RET>

We should see three records on the data base.

```
00001    AAA    Rakes      30    3.50    25
00002    BBB    Hoes       30    4.50    25
00003    CCC    Shovels    30    5.00    25
```

The first record tells us that product code AAA is rakes, we have 30 in stock, our purchase price is $3.50, and we reorder when the stock on hand gets below 25. We have 30 hoes in stock (product code BBB), each costing $4.50, and we reorder when stock gets below 25. Product code CCC is shovels, we have 30 in stock, each costs us $5.00, and we reorder when stock is below 25.

Now let's create a data base to keep track of new stock received. We'll call it NEWSTOCK, so use the command

    CREATE B:NEWSTOCK   <RET>

to create it. Structure it like so:

```
ENTER RECORD STRUCTURE AS FOLLOWS:
FIELD    NAME,TYPE,WIDTH,DECIMAL PLACES
001      CODE,C,5
002      QTY,N,5,0
003      PRICE,N,12,2
004      DATE,C,8
005
```

When dBASE asks INPUT DATA NOW? (Y/N), say Y. Let's assume we've just received two orders from our wholesalers, one order of ten rakes, each costing $4.00, and another order for six shovels, each costing $4.50. Furthermore, let's assume that we received them on March 1, 1983. To add these new items to NEWSTOCK, we'd need to type in the following data:

Code	Qty	Price	Date
AAA	10	4.00	03/01/83
BBB	6	4.50	03/01/83

When dBASE asks for data from record 3 press <RET>, and the dot prompt will appear. So if we now

    USE B:NEWSTOCK   <RET>
    LIST   <RET>

we see our new stock listed in our data base format.

```
00001    AAA        10       4.00      03/01/83
00002    BBB         6       4.50      03/01/83
```

Now we need to come up with a method to update the master inventory so that it reflects the new goods received.

Updating Data Bases with UPDATE

The dBASE UPDATE command allows us to update the contents of one data base based upon information from another. We can specify that the update either add quantities or replace entire fields. This is best explained with an example. Suppose we wish to add the new stock items to our MASTER file. Furthermore, if there is a change in the price we are paying for an item, we want the MASTER file to record the new price. In that case, we need to replace the existing price in the MASTER file with the price in the NEWSTOCK file.

Let's review what we have on both files first. If we

```
USE B:MASTER    <RET>
LIST   <RET>
```

we see our original inventory.

```
00001   AAA   Rakes     30   3.50   25
00002   BBB   Hoes      30   4.50   25
00003   CCC   Shovels   30   5.00   25
```

That is, we have 30 rakes in stock, at a wholesale price of $3.50. We have 30 hoes, wholesale priced at $4.50. We have 30 shovels, wholesale priced at $5.00. Now let's

```
USE B:NEWSTOCK   <RET>
LIST   <RET>
```

We see our new items in stock.

```
00001   AAA   10   4.00   03/01/83
00002   BBB    6   4.50   03/01/83
```

We've received ten product AAA (rakes) at $4.00 each. We've also received six product BBB (hoes) at $4.50 each. So we need to add these items to our inventory, and note that the wholesale price of rakes has increased from $3.50 to $4.00. Here is the procedure to do so.

First we must specify the *key field*, that is, the field that specifies how the update is to be performed. Both files, MASTER and NEW-STOCK, must have this field in common. In this example, CODE is the key field, because we want dBASE to add ten items of product code AAA to the master file, and six of product code BBB. dBASE will first locate product code AAA on the master file (MASTER), then search the transaction file (NEWSTOCK) for all AAAs and update MASTER's data based on the data of NEWSTOCK. Then dBASE will encounter product code BBB on the MASTER file, and search the NEWSTOCK file for all BBBs, and so forth. Let's try it out.

    USE B:MASTER   <RET>

Then type in the command

    UPDATE ON CODE FROM B:NEWSTOCK;
       ADD QTY REPLACE PRICE   <RET>

In English, this command says, "Update the MASTER file from the data in NEWSTOCK, using CODE as the comparison (key) field; add the quantities (QTY), and replace the price (PRICE)." When the dot prompt reappears, if we

    LIST   <RET>

we see

```
00001   AAA   Rakes     40   4.00   25
00002   BBB   Hoes      36   4.50   25
00003   CCC   Shovels   30   5.00   25
```

which is exactly as it should be. That is, there are now 40 rakes (AAA) in stock, because we've received 10. The price of rakes is now $4.00, as opposed to $3.50, because we REPLACED PRICE. There are now 36 hoes (BBB) in stock, because we received six. The price of hoes is still the $4.50. Shovels (CCC) were not affected, because the NEWSTOCK file did not have any information about shovels.

Now, let's discuss updating the MASTER file from the SALES data base. There are a couple of catches here to deal with. The first catch is the fact, as stated in the dBASE manual, that the FROM (transaction) file in an UPDATE command must be presorted by the key field. We can see that these are certainly not sorted by the key field, CODE. If we

    USE B:SALES   **<RET>**
    LIST   **<RET>**

we see

00001	AAA	Rakes	3	15.00	03/01/83
00002	BBB	Hoes	2	12.50	03/01/83
00003	CCC	Shovels	3	21.00	03/01/83
00004	AAA	Rakes	2	10.00	03/01/83
00005	CCC	Shovels	4	26.50	03/01/83
00006	AAA	Rakes	2	11.00	03/02/83
00007	CCC	Shovels	1	7.50	03/02/83
00008	BBB	Hoes	2	12.50	03/01/83
00009	AAA	Rakes	5	23.50	03/02/83

We can't use INDEX in this case, so we're going to have to sort to a temporary file, then copy the information to SALES. Let's try it.

    SORT ON CODE TO B:TEMP   **<RET>**
    USE B:TEMP   **<RET>**
    COPY TO B:SALES   **<RET>**
    USE B:SALES   **<RET>**
    LIST   **<RET>**

Now we see the inventory sorted by product code.

00001	AAA	Rakes	3	15.00	03/01/83
00002	AAA	Rakes	2	10.00	03/01/83
00003	AAA	Rakes	2	11.00	03/02/83
00004	AAA	Rakes	5	23.50	03/02/83
00005	BBB	Hoes	2	12.50	03/01/83
00006	BBB	Hoes	2	12.50	03/02/83
00007	CCC	Shovels	3	21.00	03/01/83
00008	CCC	Shovels	4	26.50	03/01/83
00009	CCC	Shovels	1	7.50	03/02/83

Here's the second catch. The UPDATE command allows us to *add* or replace fields in the MASTER file. However, in this case, we need to *subtract* the sales from the inventory. Since there is no SUBTRACT option with update, we're going to have to improvise. Luckily, the rules of mathematics state that if we add a negative number to a positive number, the result is subtraction. That is, 10 + (–5) is 5. So, we'll need to change all the quantities in the SALES file to negative numbers before doing the update in order for them to be subtracted from the MASTER file. We can do this with one command.

> REPLACE ALL QTY WITH – 1 * QTY   < RET >

That means, "Replace all the quantities in the SALES file with the –1 times the present value, thereby making all the quantities negative." When we LIST, we see

00001	AAA	Rakes	– 3	15.00	03/01/83
00002	AAA	Rakes	– 2	10.00	03/01/83
00003	AAA	Rakes	– 2	11.00	03/02/83
00004	AAA	Rakes	– 5	23.50	03/02/83
00005	BBB	Hoes	– 2	12.50	03/01/83
00006	BBB	Hoes	– 2	12.50	03/02/83
00007	CCC	Shovels	– 3	21.00	03/01/83
00008	CCC	Shovels	– 4	26.50	03/01/83
00009	CCC	Shovels	– 1	7.50	03/02/83

Now if we

> USE B:MASTER   < RET >
> UPDATE ON CODE FROM B:SALES ADD QTY   < RET >
> LIST   < RET >

the result on the screen will be

00001	AAA	Rakes	28	4.00	25
00002	BBB	Hoes	32	4.50	25
00003	CCC	Shovels	22	5.00	25

There are now 28 rakes in stock, because we've sold 12. There are 32 hoes, because we've sold 4, and 22 shovels, because we've sold 8.

dBASE has subtracted the quantities in the SALES file from the MASTER inventory file.

If we want information about what we need to reorder from MASTER, we

```
USE B:MASTER   <RET>
LIST FOR QTY < REORDER   <RET>
```

The result is

```
00003   CCC   Shovels   22   5.00   25
```

The amount of shovels in stock (22) has fallen below the reorder point (25).

We have a managerial problem on our hands now. Our master file is accurate, but SALES and NEWSTOCK still have data in them. If we were to add new records to these transaction data bases and do another update, our master file would then be incorrect. It would add or subtract these items a second time from our MASTER file. Therefore, we must come up with a managerial scheme for getting rid of data we've already updated. If we wished to update our MASTER file daily, a good approach might be to do the following:

1. Use the NEWSTOCK and SALES files during the course of the day to record goods received and sold.

2. At the end of the day, print a REPORT of all sales and goods received from the SALES and NEWSTOCK files for a permanent record.

3. UPDATE the MASTER file from the SALES and NEWSTOCK files.

4. DELETE and PACK all records from the SALES and NEWSTOCK file, so future updates are not confused with previous updates.

The disadvantage to this approach is that we lose all the data from the SALES and NEWSTOCK files. Here's a better approach, which leaves the SALES and NEWSTOCK files intact. Let's use NEWSTOCK as the example. Suppose on March 2 we receive 10 rakes at $4.00 each. Let's

```
USE B:NEWSTOCK    <RET>
APPEND    <RET>
```

and add the following information:

RECORD 00003

CODE :AAA :

QTY   :10:

PRICE :4.00:

DATE :03/02/83:

When we LIST, we'll see the new record added at the bottom.

```
00001   AAA   10   4.00   03/01/83
00002   BBB    6   4.50   03/01/83
00003   AAA   10   4.00   03/02/83
```

When we do another UPDATE, we won't want records 1 and 2 to be used again. So we could move only our newest entry to a file named B:TEMP.

```
COPY TO B:TEMP FOR DATE = '03/02/83'    <RET>
```

If we now

```
USE B:TEMP    <RET>
LIST    <RET>
```

we'll see

```
00003   AAA   10   4.00   03/02/83
```

Now we can update the MASTER file from TEMP, without worrying about updating records 1 and 2 again. That is, we can

```
USE B:MASTER    <RET>
UPDATE ON CODE FROM B:TEMP ADD QTY REPLACE
    PRICE    <RET>
```

When we LIST the MASTER file now, we'll see

00001	AAA	Rakes	38	4.00	25
00002	BBB	Hoes	32	4.50	25
00003	CCC	Shovels	22	5.00	25

Ten rakes have been added to the inventory. Our NEWSTOCK file still contains records of all goods received.

In this chapter, we've seen how we can design a series of data bases to manage a small business inventory. We stored individual sales and new stock items on transaction files, and used the UPDATE command to keep the master file up to date. In the next chapter, we'll explore other methods for managing multiple data bases.

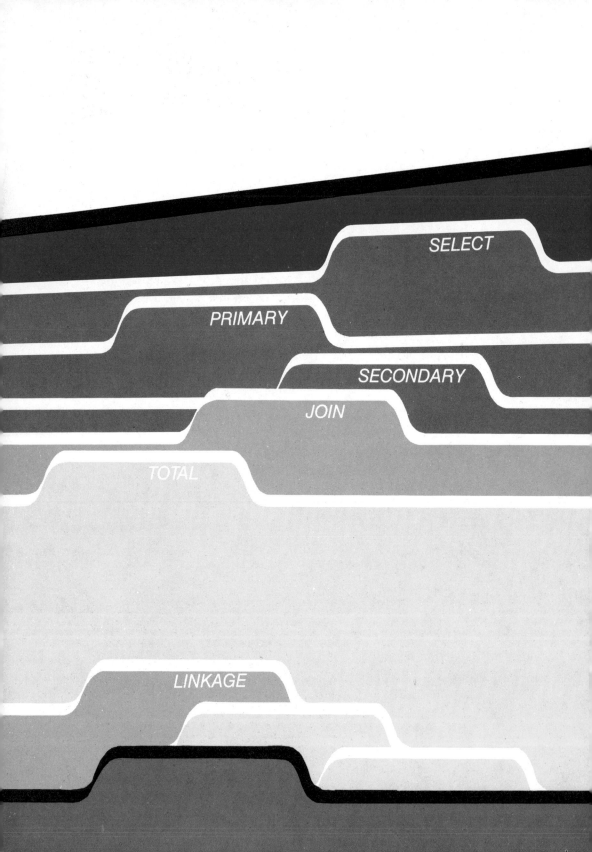

COMBINING AND SUMMARIZING DATA BASES

9

We can create a new data base using parts of two separate data bases. To do so, we need two data bases in use at the same time. We use the SELECT PRIMARY and SELECT SECONDARY commands to use two data bases at the same time.

Primary and Secondary Data Bases

With the dBASE dot prompt showing on the screen, let's designate the MASTER file as the primary data base in use.

> **SELECT PRIMARY** <RET>
> **USE B:MASTER** <RET>

Now, let's define NEWSTOCK as the secondary data base.

> **SELECT SECONDARY** <RET>
> **USE B:NEWSTOCK** <RET>

We can now refer to the data bases as simply PRIMARY or SEC-ONDARY. For example, type in

> **SELECT PRIMARY** <RET>

and ask dBASE to display the structure of the primary-use data base

> **DISPLAY STRUCTURE** <RET>

We now see

```
STRUCTURE FOR FILE: MASTER.DBF
NUMBER OF RECORDS: 00003
DATE OF LAST UPDATE: 00/00/00
PRIMARY USE DATABASE
```

FLD	NAME	TYPE	WIDTH	DEC
001	CODE	C	005	
002	TITLE	C	015	
003	QTY	N	005	
004	PRICE	N	012	002
005	REORDER	N	005	
** TOTAL **			00043	

MASTER.DBF is primary. We can also look at its contents. If we

> **LIST** <RET>

we see it contains

00001	AAA	Rakes	38	4.00	25
00002	BBB	Hoes	32	4.50	25
00003	CCC	Shovels	22	5.00	25

Now let's take a look at our secondary data base, NEWSTOCK. Type

> **SELECT SECONDARY** **<RET>**

and ask dBASE to show us the structure of the data base:

> **DISPLAY STRUCTURE** **<RET>**

We see

```
STRUCTURE FOR FILE: NEWSTOCK.DBF
NUMBER OF RECORDS: 00003
DATE OF LAST UPDATE: 00/00/00
SECONDARY USE DATABASE
```

FLD	NAME	TYPE	WIDTH	DEC
001	CODE	C	005	
002	QTY	N	005	
003	PRICE	N	012	002
004	DATE	C	008	
* * TOTAL * *			00031	

In the fourth line of the display, we are informed that this is currently a SECONDARY USE DATABASE. To see its contents, we

> **LIST** **<RET>**

and get

```
00001   AAA      10      4.00   03/01/83
00002   BBB       6      4.50   03/01/83
00003   AAA      10      4.00   03/02/83
```

Our data bases have some common field names (CODE, QTY, PRICE). Let's try a little experiment here with the primary and secondary files. First of all, let's ask dBASE to

> **DISPLAY** **<RET>**

We see

```
00003   AAA      10      4.00   03/02/83
```

the third record in NEWSTOCK. If we now

    SELECT PRIMARY   <RET>
    DISPLAY   <RET>

we see the third record in MASTER.

00003   CCC   Shovels   22   5.00   25

We're now at the bottom of these data files because the LIST command positioned us there after listing each record. At this point we
can ask dBASE for the code, quantity, and price from the third
record of the MASTER file.

    ? CODE,QTY,PRICE   <RET>

We see

CCC   22   5.00

the code, quantity, and price from the MASTER (primary) file. We
can refer to these same fields on the secondary data base by preceding the field names with an S:

    ? S.CODE,S.QTY,S.PRICE   <RET>

which gives us the result

AAA   10   4.00

the code, quantity, and price from the third record of the NEW-
STOCK file. The S. is only necessary when the two data bases have
identical field names. Hence the command

    ? DATE   <RET>

displays the date from the third record of NEWSTOCK.

03/02/83

The secondary file was assumed because the primary file has no
DATE field. Now, keeping these relationships in mind, we can create
a third data base, using parts of these two, with the JOIN command.

Combining Two Data Bases with JOIN

Suppose we wanted a data base that had all of NEWSTOCK's information on it, but also had the title for each product code. Since NEWSTOCK does not contain this information, we need to get it from MASTER. One method for doing this would be to create a third data base with some information from each of the two files. The JOIN command can be used for this.

When we combine two data bases, we must assign a name to the newly created file. The data bases to be combined must have some common characteristic (a key field). We can also define the fields that we want on the third data base. The command

        JOIN TO B:NEWDB FOR CODE = S.CODE FIELD CODE,TITLE,;
            S.QTY,S.PRICE,DATE   <RET>

says, "Join the primary and secondary data bases to a new data base called NEWDB, use CODE as the key field. NEWDB will have the fields CODE, TITLE, S.QTY, S.PRICE, and DATE."

If we now wish to look at the structure of NEWDB, we type

        USE B:NEWDB   <RET>
        DISPLAY STRUCTURE   <RET>

We see that it has five fields: CODE, TITLE, QTY, PRICE, and DATE.

STRUCTURE FOR FILE: NEWDB.DBF

NUMBER OF RECORDS: 00003

DATE OF LAST UPDATE: 32/32/32

PRIMARY USE DATABASE

FLD	NAME	TYPE	WIDTH	DEC
001	CODE	C	005	
002	TITLE	C	015	
003	QTY	N	005	
004	PRICE	N	012	002
005	DATE	C	008	
* * TOTAL * *			00046	

Look at its contents by typing

LIST   <RET>

We see that it contains

00001	AAA	Rakes	10	4.00	03/01/83
00002	AAA	Rakes	10	4.00	03/02/83
00003	BBB	Hoes	6	4.50	03/01/83

the data from NEWSTOCK, with the additional TITLE field which was taken from MASTER. The titles are correct for the product codes, because we joined FOR CODE=S.CODE (primary data base CODE equal to secondary data base code, S.CODE). Where the CODE field from the primary data base matches the CODE field from secondary, so will the other fields.

JOIN is a very powerful command, and mastering it takes some practice. We'll see another way to combine data from two data bases in a moment. First, let's discuss how to condense information in summary form.

Summarizing Data Bases with TOTAL

We can summarize data in a data base using the TOTAL command. For example, suppose the end of March rolls around, and we want to get a summary view of how much we sold. To find out, we could USE the sales data base and total up all the sales by code. That is, if we

USE B:SALES   <RET>
LIST   <RET>

we see

00001	AAA	Rakes	−3	15.00	03/01/83
00002	AAA	Rakes	−2	10.00	03/01/83
00003	AAA	Rakes	−2	11.00	03/02/83

00004	AAA	Rakes	−5	23.50	03/02/83
00005	BBB	Shovels	−2	12.50	03/02/83
00006	BBB	Shovels	−2	12.50	03/02/83
00007	CCC	Hoes	−3	21.00	03/01/83
00008	CCC	Hoes	−4	26.50	03/01/83
00009	CCC	Hoes	−1	7.50	03/02/83

Whoops. We still have negative numbers in our data base from the work we did a chapter ago. Let's replace all the negative numbers with positive numbers for this example:

REPLACE ALL QTY WITH −1∗QTY   <RET>
LIST   <RET>

Now we'll see

00001	AAA	Rakes	3	15.00	03/01/83
00002	AAA	Rakes	2	10.00	03/01/83
00003	AAA	Rakes	2	11.00	03/02/83
00004	AAA	Rakes	5	23.50	03/02/83
00005	BBB	Shovels	2	12.50	03/02/83
00006	BBB	Shovels	2	12.50	03/02/83
00007	CCC	Hoes	3	21.00	03/01/83
00008	CCC	Hoes	4	26.50	03/01/83
00009	CCC	Hoes	1	7.50	03/02/83

That's better. Now we can create a summary data base which will tell us the total quantity and amount of each product sold for the month. We'll use the TOTAL command. There is one rule that we must bear in mind when we TOTAL. The data base must be either already sorted by the key field, or indexed by the key field. We can see that our data base is already sorted by the key field (CODE), so we just need to

TOTAL ON CODE TO B:SALESUMM FIELD CODE,TITLE,;
QTY,AMOUNT   <RET>

This says, "Total the product codes to a new data base called SALE-SUMM. Put the CODE, TITLE, QTY, and AMOUNT fields on the new data base." After typing in this command, we'll get the message

00003 RECORDS COPIED

and the dot prompt back. If we now use the new data base

    USE B:SALESUMM   <RET>
    LIST   <RET>

we see

00001	AAA	Rakes	12	59.50
00002	BBB	Hoes	4	25.00
00003	CCC	Shovels	8	55.00

a summary of all the data on SALES. That is, we've sold 12 rakes for a total of $59.50. We've sold four hoes for $25.00, and eight shovels for a total of $55.00.

Now, suppose we want a report that tells us all this information, plus average unit price, profit margin from sales, and the quantity of each item left in stock. Obviously, we're going to have to get some data from the MASTER file to do so. However, we need not use the JOIN command. We'll just produce a REPORT which takes data from both data bases.

Printing a Report from Two Data Bases

We have a unique situation with our SALESUMM and MASTER data bases. That is, they are in exactly the same order. Let's

    USE B:MASTER
    LIST   <RET>

On the screen is the result:

0000i	AAA	Rakes	28	4.00	25
00002	BBB	Hoes	32	4.50	25
00003	CCC	Shovels	22	5.00	25

When we

    USE B:SALESUMM   <RET>
    LIST   <RET>

we see

00001	AAA	Rakes	12	59.50
00002	BBB	Hoes	4	25.00
00003	CCC	Shovels	8	55.00

Each has three records, and each is in the order AAA, BBB, CCC. When two data bases have a relationship like this, we can create a REPORT using data from both data bases. Here's how to do it.

    First, we must again define primary and secondary data bases. To do this, we

    SELECT PRIMARY   <RET>
    USE B:MASTER   <RET>
    SELECT SECONDARY   <RET>
    USE B:SALESUMM   <RET>
    SET LINKAGE ON   <RET>

By setting linkage on, we inform dBASE that we will be stepping through the two data bases uniformly. That is, we'll use record 1 from both data bases, then skip down to record 2 in both data bases, then skip down to record 3 in both data bases. Any movement through one data base will create the same movement through the other. Now let's design a report format called INVSUMM (Inventory Summary).

    REPORT FORM B:INVSUMM   <RET>

We'll give it this format:

ENTER OPTIONS (M = RIGHT MARGIN, L = LINES/PAGE,
    W = WIDTH)M = 1,W = 80
PAGE HEADING? (Y/N) Y
ENTER PAGE HEADING: Summary Report of Inventory and Sales
DOUBLE SPACE REPORT? (Y/N) N
ARE TOTALS REQUIRED? (Y/N) Y

```
SUBTOTALS IN REPORT? (Y/N) N
COL    WIDTH,CONTENTS
001    5,CODE
ENTER HEADING: Code
002    15,Title
ENTER HEADING: Description
003    5,S.QTY
ENTER HEADING: Units Sold
ARE TOTALS REQUIRED? (Y/N) Y
004    8,AMOUNT/S.QTY
ENTER HEADING: Average Price
ARE TOTALS REQUIRED? (Y/N) Y
005    8,PRICE
ENTER HEADING: Our Cost
ARE TOTALS REQUIRED? (Y/N) Y
006    8,(AMOUNT/S.QTY)-PRICE
ENTER HEADING: Margin
ARE TOTALS REQUIRED? (Y/N) Y
007    5,P.QTY
ENTER HEADING: On Hand
ARE TOTALS REQUIRED? (Y/N) Y
008
```

We just press < RET > for field 8, and we get the following report:

```
PAGE NO. 00001
03/31/83
```

Summary Report of Inventory and Sales

Code	Description	Units Sold	Average Price	Our Cost	Margin	On Hand
AAA	Rakes	12	4.95	4.00	0.95	38
BBB	Hoes	4	6.25	4.50	1.75	32
CCC	Shovels	8	6.87	5.00	1.87	22
** TOTAL **						
		24	18.08	13.50	4.58	92

Let's look at the row for rakes. In the first column is CODE, second column is TITLE, third column is the quantity sold from SALESUMM (S.QTY). Then, the average selling price from SALESUMM (S.QTY/AMOUNT) is in the fourth column. The fifth column is the wholesale price (PRICE from the MASTER file). The sixth column is the profit margin ((S.QTY/AMOUNT)-PRICE). The seventh column is the quantity on hand from the MASTER file (P.QTY). We needed to use P.QTY because both data bases have a QTY field. The P. means the primary data base's QTY field.

The report provides a great deal of information at a glance. By combining data from the MASTER file and the summarized SALES file on the report, we can see how many of each item was sold, the average price that each was sold at, our cost per item, our profit margin, and the quantity still in stock.

As we can see, there is much we can do with multiple data files in dBASE. The commands we've discussed here do a great deal of work, and therefore require more study and thinking than do simpler commands like CREATE and LIST. Acquiring the skills to fully manage several data bases and more complex commands takes some practice, but we now have some techniques to do so. The dBASE II user's manual provides more examples of the various commands, but as with all aspects of learning to use computers, you will learn best by trying them.

Starting with the next chapter, we will begin to explore another facet of dBASE II, command files. But first we must get a feel for the computer's main memory (RAM) and memory variables.

A computer's main memory is called *random access memory*, or *RAM*. All of this memory is available when the computer is turned on; whatever was stored in RAM is lost when you shut off the power. With dBASE II, we can store data in the temporary RAM similar to the way we store data in fields of data bases on disk. Data in fields have field names. Data in RAM also have names, which are stored in *memory variables* instead of data bases. Memory variables are temporary storage places for pieces of information you are using while working out a problem. In dBASE II, you can store 64 of these variables. The name you use for a memory variable can be up to ten characters. Let's start by getting a good feel for memory variables by examining the arithmetic capabilities of RAM.

Managing Data in RAM

Using RAM memory in your computer is much like using any pocket calculator. We ask dBASE to calculate some numbers, and it displays the answer. Let's load up dBASE and get the dot prompt to show on the screen. Then let's put the computer's main memory (RAM) to work. Next to the dot prompt, type in this command:

    ? 1 + 1   < RET >

dBASE responds with

2

the sum of 1 plus 1. Let's give it a tougher problem. Let's ask dBASE to

    ? 25/5   < RET >

It responds with

5

the quotient of 25 divided by 5. Not bad. dBASE is performing as well as our $5.00 calculator.

Now we can give it an even tougher problem. Suppose we need to know what the cost of an item selling for $181.93 is if we must pay 6% sales tax. That is, we need to know how much 181.93 + 6% of 181.93 is. Type in

    ? 181.93 + (.06 * 181.93)   < RET >

dBASE tells us that the total cost is

192.8458

The four decimal places give us more accuracy than necessary, but it beats paper and pencil.

We can also work with non-numeric data (called *character strings* or just *strings*) in RAM too. For instance, if we type in

? 'Hi' + 'There'   < RET>

we get the result

Hithere

Notice when we "added" two strings, they were linked together rather than summed. At first you might think that dBASE was naturally clever enough to figure this out on its own, but it was not dBASE's idea. Rather, it was the fact that we enclosed "hi" and "there" in apostrophes that told dBASE to link rather than sum. So does this mean that if we enclose the ones in 1+1 in apostrophes, it will also link rather than sum? Try it. Type in

? '1' + '1'   < RET>

and, yes, dBASE responds with

11

two ones linked together, not summed. Interesting. The apostrophes told dBASE to treat the ones as character strings, not as numbers. This leaves us another possibility: to print hi + there without the apostrophes. Type in

? hi + there   < RET>

dBASE informs us that it can't perform this operation. It says

* * * SYNTAX ERROR * * *
   ?
? HI + there
CORRECT AND RETRY (Y/N)?

Hmmmm. It looks like these apostrophes carry quite a bit of meaning in RAM. There is a very good reason for this, as we shall see in a moment. For now, keep in mind that if we wish to do math with numbers, we do not use apostrophes (i.e. 1 + 1). If we wish to link strings together, we must use apostrophes (i.e. ? 'hi ' + 'there').

Now let's explore the reason for the syntax error that occurred when we attempted to ? hi + there without the apostrophes.

Storing Data to Memory Variables with STORE

How do we store data in memory variables? First, we pick a name for the memory variable, and ask dBASE to store some information in it. A variable in the computer sense is exactly the same as a variable in the mathematical sense. That is, if we know that variable $X = 10$, and variable $Y = 5$, then we know that $X + Y = 15$. The same is true with computers. In order to store a value (such as 10) to a variable (such as X), we use the STORE command. Let's name our first variable X, and store 10 under that name.

STORE 10 TO X   <RET>

dBASE displays the brief message

10

Now let's create another variable name, Y, and store 5 under that name:

STORE 5 TO Y   <RET>

dBASE displays

5

When we ask dBASE for the sum of $X + Y$, like so:

? X+Y   <RET>

it should respond with 15, which it does.

15

While the variables are invisible to us right now, we can take a look at them by typing in the command to

DISPLAY MEMORY   <RET>

and dBASE displays our variable names and what we've stored in them.

X	(N)	10
Y	(N)	5
* * TOTAL * *		02 VARIABLES USED 00012 BYTES USED

It informs us that two memory variables exist: X and Y. Furthermore, we know that each is numeric (N), and that the value of X is 10 and the value of Y is 5. Since they are numeric, we can do basic math with them. For example, we can subtract them:

> ? X – Y   <RET>

and get the result

5

which is the difference of 10 – 5. To multiply them, we type

> ? X*Y   <RET>

We get the product

50

ten times five. If we wish to divide the numbers stored in the memory variables, we type

> ? X/Y   <RET>

We get the quotient

2

the answer to ten divided by two.

   We are not limited to simple equations. For example, if we wish to get the answer to X plus Y times X, we type

> ? X + Y*X   <RET>

The result is

60

dBASE automatically follows the standard order of precedence in math computation. That is, when an equation involves both multiplication and addition, the multiplication is performed first. We can alter the order of computations by using parentheses.

    ? (X + Y)*X   <RET>

We get the result

150

In this case, the addition was performed first. At this point, we have stored data to two memory variables, X and Y. So if we ask dBASE to

    ? A + B   <RET>

we get an error

    * * * SYNTAX ERROR * * *
      ?
    ? A + B
    CORRECT AND RETRY (Y/N)?

because we've asked dBASE to sum A and B, variables we have not yet used for storing data.
    If we again examine our memory variables by typing

    DISPLAY MEMORY   <RET>

we see that we have numbers stored in X and Y.

    X   (N)   10
    Y   (N)   5
    * * TOTAL * *   02 VARIABLES USED 00012 BYTES USED

A while back we got a syntax error when we asked dBASE to ? hi + there. That is because memory variables "hi" and "there" do not exist. Of course, we could create a couple of memory variables called HI and THERE. That is, we can

    STORE 'Hello' TO HI   <RET>

and then

    STORE ' yourself' TO THERE   < RET >

Now we can type in the command

    ? HI + THERE   < RET >

and dBASE will respond with

Hello yourself

That is, the contents of memory variables HI and THERE linked together. Why are they linked? Let's see what we have stored in our memory variables.

    DISPLAY MEMORY   < RET >

Now we have four memory variables.

X	(N)	10
Y	(N)	5
HI	(C)	Hello
THERE	(C)	yourself
* * TOTAL * *		04 VARIABLES USED 00025 BYTES USED

Memory variables HI and THERE are of the character (C) type. We told dBASE they were character types by putting apostrophes around them when we stored them (STORE 'Hello' TO HI). Notice an important difference between fields and memory variables here. When we define types of data in fields, we specifically state C or N when we CREATE the data base. In memory variables, dBASE automatically assumes that data stored without apostrophes (STORE 10 TO X) are numbers, and data stored with apostrophes (STORE 'Hello' TO HI) are characters.

    If we wish to link the words "hi" and "there," rather than asking for the contents of the memory variables HI and THERE, we use apostrophes.

    ? 'Hi' + ' there'   < RET >

This gives us the result

Hi there

on the screen. The apostrophes told dBASE that we want to link the words 'Hi' and ' there' literally. To use the same principle with X and Y, if we were to ask dBASE to

    ? X+Y   <RET>

we'd get

15

as the answer, the sum of numeric variable X (10) plus numeric variable Y (5). On the other hand, if we use apostrophes,

    ? 'X' + 'Y'   <RET>

we get

XY

This is literally an X and a Y linked together.

The important aspect of memory variables you should remember is that they are not permanent like field data are. RAM memory is temporary. Disk storage is permanent. When we QUIT dBASE and turn off our computer, our data bases are still safe and sound on disk. However, memory variables are erased completely. Memory variables are available as a sort of computer scratch pad, as we will see in the coming chapters.

MODIFY COMMAND

DO

DO WHILE ... ENDDO

EOF

SKIP

GO TOP

GO BOTTOM

RETURN

CREATING COMMAND FILES

11

A *command file* is a disk file that has a series of commands in it. We record commands in files because it is more convenient to have dBASE do a whole batch of commands than for us to type in each command one at a time. The potential of command files goes far beyond saving time, however, as we shall see. A command file is actually a computer program, and from now on we'll use the words command file and program interchangeably.

A *computer program* is similar to the program we receive when we go to the theatre. The theater's program displays the series of events that are to be carried out, and the order in which they will occur. Likewise, the computer program presents a series of commands to the computer in the order in which they are to be carried out. Of course, the computer program is more difficult to read than the theater program because it is not in plain English. It is written in a computer language. In this book, our programs will be written in dBASE II, the computer language that we're already familiar with.

The basic procedure for working with command files goes something like this. First, we write the command file, and save it using a filename. Then, we run the command file by asking dBASE to DO the command file. Sometimes we make mistakes when we create a command file, so then we have to edit it. Correcting these errors is called *debugging*. Let's deal with creating command files first.

Creating Command Files with MODIFY

Remember our mailing list from the first five chapters? We were able to do some pretty fancy things with it, like LIST and SORT and EDIT. However, we never had a chance to print mailing labels from it. This is because dBASE doesn't have a command to print mailing labels. When dBASE doesn't have a command to do some task we want, we have to write a command file to do it.

Let's write a mailing label command file now. Use the disk that we put our MAIL.DBF data base on as the disk in drive B. We'll call our command file LABELS, and we'll store it on the disk in drive B too. The command to create a new command file, or edit an existing one, is MODIFY COMMAND plus the name of the command file. So let's ask dBASE to

    MODIFY COMMAND B:LABELS   <RET>

dBASE informs us that this is a

NEW FILE

then gives us a blank screen on which to write our command file.

Let's go ahead and type it in. Make sure you type it exactly as it appears on the page here, or it may not work properly when you run it.

```
? TRIM(FNAME),LNAME
? ADDRESS
? TRIM(CITY)+', '+STATE+ZIP
```

Press the RETURN key after typing in each line to get down to the next blank line. If you make errors while you're typing in the program, you can move the cursor around to make changes. The cursor control keys are the same as we use in the EDIT and APPEND modes. Once you have it typed in exactly as above, save it by typing in a ^W.

We have just written our first command file, and stored it on the disk in drive B as LABELS.CMD. (As you've probably guessed, dBASE added the .CMD, which stands for command file. The MS-DOS and PC-DOS operating systems add the extension .PRG, which stands for program.) Now let's run our program.

Running Command Files with DO

First of all, let's tell dBASE to use the MAIL as the data base.

```
USE B:MAIL   <RET>
```

Now to run our command file, we need to tell dBASE to

```
DO B:LABELS   <RET>
```

and we see on the screen

```
Andy Appleby
345 Oak St.
Los Angeles, CA 92123
```

dBASE did all three lines in the command file in the order they were placed. That is, dBASE printed the first name with the blanks trimmed off followed by the last name (? TRIM(FNAME),LNAME). Then it printed the address (? ADDRESS), then the city, followed by a comma, the state and the zip (? TRIM(CITY) + ',' + STATE + ZIP). This is the first mailing label.

Let's review the steps. We created the command file, using the MODIFY COMMAND command, and called it LABELS.CMD. We saved the command file, using a ^W. When the dot prompt reappeared, we asked dBASE to DO B:LABELS. dBASE then did each of the commands in the command file in the order in which they appeared. That is, dBASE read the command file left to right, top to bottom, just as we read English. The results came out in that order.

This is not bad for a first command file, but we can see one major weakness right off the bat: it only prints one label. In order to get dBASE to print all the labels in the data base, we need to set up a *loop* in the command file.

Setting Up Loops in Programs with DO WHILE and ENDDO

dBASE has a pair of commands called DO WHILE and ENDDO which can be used in a program to repeat a series of commands indefinitely. All we have to do is enclose the commands to be repeated between a DO WHILE and an ENDDO command. Every DO WHILE begins a loop, and must have an ENDDO command to end it. We also need to tell dBASE what the condition is for performing the commands inside the loop. Let's give it a try in our LABELS program. First we'll ask dBASE to

    MODIFY COMMAND B:LABELS   <RET>

at which point dBASE will redisplay LABELS.CMD on the screen and let us make some changes. We see this on the screen:

? TRIM(FNAME),LNAME

? ADDRESS

? TRIM(CITY) + ', ' + STATE + ZIP

To make dBASE print labels for every person in the mailing list, we need to put these commands inside a loop. So, type a ^N to make room for a new line, and add the DO WHILE command at the top, as shown below.

You will also need to add a SKIP command to have dBASE skip down to the next name in the data base as it performs the commands in the loop. Then we need an ENDDO to end the loop. Finally, a RETURN command will tell dBASE to return to the dot prompt after the program is done. Let's type in this command file:

```
DO WHILE .NOT. EOF
? TRIM(FNAME),LNAME
? ADDRESS
? TRIM(CITY)+', '+STATE+ZIP
SKIP
ENDDO
RETURN
```

Now save the edited version of the command file with a ^W. When the dot prompt reappears, let's

```
USE B:MAIL    <RET>
DO B:LABELS   <RET>
```

and we get

```
Andy Appleby
345 Oak St.
Los Angeles, CA 92123
RECORD 00001

John Q. Smith
123 A. St.
San Diego, CA 92123
RECORD 00002

Lucy Smithsonian
461 Adams St.
San Diego, CA 92122-1234
RECORD 00003

Ruth Doe
1142 J. St.
```

Los Angeles, CA 91234
RECORD 00004

Betsy SMITH
222 Lemon Dr.
New York, NY 01234
RECORD 00005

If something goes wrong when you try this, check to see if you typed it in exactly as it appears in the book. If your program seems to be running on and on endlessly, press the escape (ESC) key on your keyboard to cancel the run and get back to the dot prompt. Then, you'll need to MODIFY COMMAND B:LABELS again, and make the appropriate corrections so that it *exactly* matches the LABELS.CMD program in the book.

Now all the names on the data base are on the screen in a mailing label format. Let's summarize what we did here. In the command file, we told dBASE to DO WHILE .NOT. EOF. In English, this translates to, "Do everything between here and the ENDDO command as long as you haven't reached the EOF, end of the data base file." The next three lines in the command file then print one label. Then the SKIP command causes dBASE to SKIP down to the next record in the data base. The ENDDO command marks the end of the loop, but the loop is repeated because the end of the file (EOF) has not been reached yet. Hence, another label is printed, dBASE skips down to the next name and address, and another label is printed, until all the labels have been printed. At that point dBASE has reached the end of the data base. This causes the loop to end and the first command under the ENDDO command to be processed, then to return. The RETURN command simply tells dBASE to RETURN to the dot prompt in this case.

One problem with our mailing labels is that they have record numbers on them. We can get rid of the record numbers by asking dBASE to SET TALK OFF. Let's run the program again. This time, let's first

    USE B:MAIL <RET>

then, tell dBASE to get rid of the record numbers with

    SET TALK OFF <RET>

If you have a printer hooked up, you can also

    SET PRINT ON   <RET>

Now let's run our LABELS program. Tell dBASE to

    DO B:LABELS   <RET>

and we see on the printer (or screen, if you don't have a printer) that the record numbers have been removed.

Andy Appleby

345 Oak St.

Los Angeles, CA 92123

John Q. Smith

123 A. St.

San Diego, CA 92123

Lucy Smithsonian

461 Adams St.

San Diego, CA 92122-1234

Ruth Doe

1142 J. St.

Los Angeles, CA 91234

Betsy SMITH

222 Lemon Dr.

New York, NY 01234

    If you did SET PRINT ON, I suggest that you now type in the command to

    SET PRINT OFF   <RET>

otherwise everything else that you type on the screen will go to your printer too.

    We've got a little problem here. Most mailing labels are one inch tall, and the names are spaced evenly on each one. It just so happens that most printers print six lines to the inch, so if we modify our command file to print six lines for each label, each name and address should fit perfectly on one label. So let's

> MODIFY COMMAND B:LABELS   < RET >

Now type in four ^Xs to get the cursor on the SKIP command. Then, do three ^Ns to make room for three new lines, so the command file looks like this:

```
DO WHILE .NOT. EOF
? TRIM(FNAME),LNAME
? ADDRESS
? TRIM(CITY)+', '+STATE+ZIP

—


SKIP
ENDDO
RETURN
```

Now we'll put in commands to print three blank lines on each mailing label. That is, we will begin each blank line with a ? command.

```
DO WHILE .NOT. EOF
? TRIM(FNAME),LNAME
? ADDRESS
? TRIM(CITY)+', '+STATE+ZIP
?
?
?
SKIP
ENDDO
RETURN
```

Save it with a ^W. Now let's

> USE B:MAIL   < RET >
> DO B:LABELS   < RET >

and we should see the names and addresses properly formatted for 1-inch tall mailing labels.

Andy Appleby

345 Oak St.

Los Angeles, CA 92123

John Q. Smith
123 A. St.
San Diego, CA 92123

Lucy Smithsonian
461 Adams St.
San Diego, CA 92122-1234

Ruth Doe
1142 J. St.
Los Angeles, CA 91234

Betsy SMITH
222 Lemon Dr.
New York, NY 01234

Much better. The labels have the extra three blank lines between them. You may wonder why we repeatedly type in USE B:MAIL. We do so to get back to the top of the data base. If we *don't* USE our file at this point, we'll get nothing on the screen when we type DO B:LABELS. Try it.

    DO B:LABELS   **<RET>**

All we get is the dot prompt. Yet we know that there are several records in the data base. Type in the command

    DISPLAY   **<RET>**

We see one record:

00006   SMITH   Betsy   222 Lemon Dr.   New York   NY   01234

This is the last record in the data base. Let's ask dBASE if it is at the end of the data base.

    ? EOF   **<RET>**

dBASE responds with

.T.

which is dBASE's way of saying, "True, I'm at the end of the data base." Recall that in our command file, we said to print labels while we were *not* at the end of the data base (DO WHILE .NOT. EOF). So that's why when we ran our program this time, we got nothing. We can return to the top of the data base by typing

    GO TOP   <RET>

If we then type

    DO B:LABELS   <RET>

we'll see our labels. It might be to our benefit to put the GO TOP command right into the command file, so we don't have to remember to type it in ourselves every time we do LABELS. We can now add GO TOP at the top of our program.

```
GO TOP
DO WHILE .NOT. EOF
? TRIM(FNAME),LNAME
? ADDRESS
? TRIM(CITY)+', '+STATE+ZIP
?
?
?
SKIP
ENDDO
RETURN
```

Then the program will always start with dBASE at the top (first record) of the data base. Notice that the GO TOP command is outside and above the loop. This is so that dBASE will start at the first record, then start the loop. Had we put the GO TOP command inside the loop, the command file would print a label for the first record, skip to the next record, go back to the first record, print that label again, skip to the next record, back to the first record... on and on. The command file would print countless mailing labels for the first record on the data base.

Now we have a good mailing label program to use with our MAIL file. We could spruce it up a bit so that it's nicer to look at. Take a look at this version of LABELS.CMD.

```
********* Mailing Labels Program.
GO TOP

DO WHILE .NOT. EOF
    ? TRIM(FNAME),LNAME
    ? ADDRESS
    ? TRIM(CITY)+', '+STATE+ZIP
    ?
    ?
    ?
    SKIP
ENDDO
RETURN
```

Notice that we added a title. Programmers often put titles and comments in their programs as notes to themselves. The comments don't have any effect on the actual program; they're just reminders to the person who wrote it. To put comments in dBASE programs like this, we must start the line with an asterisk (∗). A lot of asterisks make the line stand out, but only one is necessary. Also note that there is a blank line between the GO TOP command and the start of the DO WHILE LOOP. This was only to make the loop stand out when looking at the program. Also, all of the commands inside of the DO WHILE loop are indented. This makes the commands inside the loop stand out even further. If you want to make your command file look like this one, just MODIFY COMMAND B:LABELS. Then, do a ^N to make room for the title and type it in. Don't forget to put at least one asterisk in front of it. Then position the cursor under the GO TOP command, and type a ^N. Then position the cursor next to the ? TRIM(FNAME) line, type a ^V (INSERT ON), and hit the space bar a few times to indent the line. Do the same for the other lines within the loop, then save it with a ^W.

In the next chapter, we'll look at another capability that we can use with our command files: decision making.

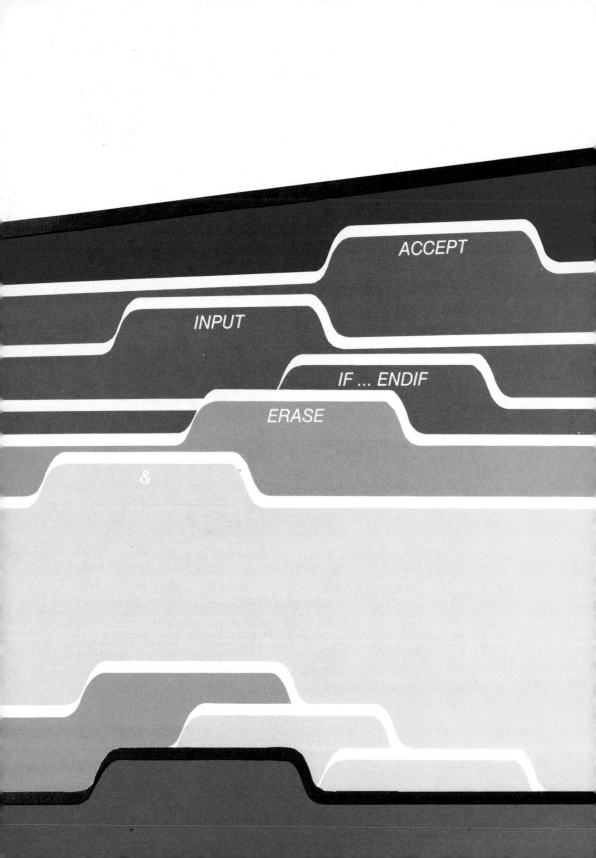

ACCEPT

INPUT

IF ... ENDIF

ERASE

&

MAKING DECISIONS

12

The LABELS program we created in the last chapter has one limitation. It always prints out labels for everyone on the data base, even though we might want labels for just San Diego residents or the 92122 zip code area. A better label program would allow us to specify only the labels we want printed. In this chapter, we'll learn to build this capability into our LABELS program.

Asking Questions with ACCEPT and INPUT

If the command file is going to print only certain labels for us, it needs to know what labels we have in mind. That is, it needs to *ask* us what labels we desire. We can make our command files ask us questions with the ACCEPT and INPUT commands. When we use either of these commands, we also type the question to be asked in apostrophes. We also need to provide a memory variable in which to store the answer to the question. We can try this out with a command file called B:TEST:

    MODIFY COMMAND B:TEST   <RET>

When the blank screen appears, type in this line:

    ACCEPT 'What is your name? ' TO NAME

and save it. Then DO B:TEST. We would see on the screen

What is your name? :

dBASE will leave the question on the screen until we type in an answer. If we type in

    FRED ASTAIRE   <RET>

the dot prompt would appear because the program is over. This isn't too exciting, but if we now ask dBASE to

    ? NAME   <RET>

we see

FRED ASTAIRE

If we were to DISPLAY MEMORY now, we'd see we have a memory variable called NAME, of the character type, with the contents FRED ASTAIRE. So we've been able to have the command file ask a question, wait for an answer, and remember the answer by storing it to a memory variable.

The INPUT command is very similar to the ACCEPT command, except that it is used when the answer to the question is a number.

For example, try making a command file called B:TEST2 that looks like this:

```
INPUT ' Enter a number ' TO ANSWER
```

Save it, then DO B:TEST2, and the request appears

Enter a number :

Type in any old number, say 999 <RET>. The dot prompt reappears. Next type

```
? ANSWER   <RET>
```

We see

999

When we DISPLAY MEMORY, we see that we have a memory variable called ANSWER, and it is numeric (N).

We'll see a practical application of the ACCEPT command in a moment.

Making Decisions with IF and ENDIF

We can embed some decision making into our command files by using the IF and ENDIF commands. IF, in dBASE, means the same thing as it does in English, i.e. "if (a condition is met), then (do something)." Each IF must be accompanied by an ENDIF. Let's look at a practical example.

Let's start by modifying the LABELS program. Let's change it so that before it prints labels, it asks us which zip code area we want labels for, then prints labels for only individuals who live in that zip code area. Here is what we should do:

```
MODIFY COMMAND B:LABELS   <RET>
```

This brings our labels program to the screen for us to edit. It should look something like the one in Program 12.1.

Now, just under the title, we need to add these three lines. The first, SET TALK off, will be used to keep the record numbers of the labels. The second, ERASE, will clear the screen. Then we'll put in an ACCEPT statement so the command file will ask us a question.

```
SET TALK off
ERASE
ACCEPT ' What zip code area ' TO AREA
```

So move the cursor down one line (^X), and do a couple of ^Ns to make room, then type in the new lines so the command file looks like Program 12.2.

```
********* Mailing Labels Program.
GO TOP

DO WHILE .NOT. EOF
    ? TRIM(FNAME),LNAME
    ? ADDRESS
    ? TRIM(CITY)+', '+STATE+ZIP
    ?
    ?
    ?
    SKIP
ENDDO
RETURN
```

—Program 12.1—

```
********* Mailing Labels Program.
SET TALK off
ERASE
ACCEPT ' What zip code area ' TO AREA
GO TOP

DO WHILE .NOT. EOF
    ? TRIM(FNAME),LNAME
    ? ADDRESS
    ? TRIM(CITY)+', '+STATE+ZIP
    ?
    ?
    ?
    SKIP
ENDDO
RETURN
```

—Program 12.2—

The ACCEPT command will present its question on the screen, then wait for an answer. It will store the answer to a memory variable named AREA. Now we need to type in two other lines, which will qualify the labels to be printed: IF ZIP=AREA and to end it, ENDIF. The first one goes right under the DO WHILE command line, and the ENDIF goes just above the SKIP command. You may want to add blank lines and indent the ? lines a little further as I have, but it is not necessary to do so. These are just for looks. In Program 12.3, you can see how the command file should look after you make these changes.

Double check to make sure you've typed in everything correctly, then save the command file with a ^W. Now, let's try it out. First, let's USE B:MAIL if you haven't already done so. Then let's

DO B:LABELS   <RET>

The first thing that should happen is that the screen clears and the following question appears:

What zip code area? :

Our command file is asking us a question, and is waiting for an answer. Let's type in 92123 <RET>. Then two labels appear on the screen.

```
******** Mailing Labels Program.
ERASE
ACCEPT ' What zip code area ' TO AREA
GO TOP

DO WHILE .NOT. EOF

    IF ZIP = AREA
        ? TRIM(FNAME),LNAME
        ? ADDRESS
        ? TRIM(CITY)+', '+STATE+ZIP
        ?
        ?
        ?
    ENDIF

    SKIP
ENDDO
RETURN
```

Program 12.3

Andy Appleby
345 Oak St.
Los Angeles, CA 92123

John Q. Smith
123 A. St.
San Diego, CA 92123

How about that? The command file asked which zip code area we wanted, then printed labels for people who live in that area. I'm impressed. Now, let's review why it did this. Let's take another look at the command file in Program 12.3.

When we asked dBASE to DO B:LABELS, it followed the instructions in our program. It ignored the title because of the leading asterisks, then it cleared the screen (ERASE), then it presented the question "What zip code area?" and waited for an answer. This is because the ACCEPT command told dBASE to present the question in the apostrophes, then wait for an answer. dBASE waited until we typed in our reply, 92123, then it stored 92123 to a memory variable called AREA. Then the program began the loop through the data base. Prior to printing each label, it checked to see IF ZIP = AREA. That is, it checked to see if the zip code on the record matched AREA, the zip code we typed in response to the "What zip code area?" question. If they matched, it printed the label. If they didn't match, all the lines between the IF and ENDIF were ignored. Either way, the SKIP command told dBASE to go to the next record. Then ENDDO sent dBASE through another loop, checking to see if the zip code on the next record matched the area we requested. It continued doing so until it got to the end of the data base.

We can DO B:LABELS again, and this time when it asks

What zip code area? :

type in 91234 <RET> and, sure enough, we get

Ruth Doe
1142 J. St.
Los Angeles, CA 91234

This is the only person on our data base in the 91234 zip code area.

We can print labels for a broader zip code area by typing in a partial zip code. If we DO B:LABELS and type in 92 as the zip code area to print labels for, we get

Andy Appleby
345 Oak St.
Los Angeles, CA 92123

John Q. Smith
123 A. St.
San Diego, CA 92123

Lucy Smithsonian
461 Adams St.
San Diego, CA 92122-1234

all the people in the 92XXX zip code areas. This feature is useful now, but it wasn't so handy in Chapter 3 when we asked for a list of Smiths and got Smithsonians in there too. dBASE listed all the 92XXX zip codes here because 9 and 2 were the first two digits of their zip codes.

Let's add the option to send mailing labels to the printer. Ask dBASE to MODIFY COMMAND B:LABELS < RET>, so we can edit it. Now, as shown in Program 12.4, add the lines I've added (the new lines are in darker print).

Once you've made the changes, save the command file with a ^W and the DO B:LABELS < RET>. This time we see

What zip code area? :

We'll type in 91234 < RET>, then we see

Shall I send labels to the printer? (Y/N)

We put in Y/N as a clue that the program is expecting a yes or no answer. If you have a printer hooked up to your computer, type in a Y< RET>. Otherwise, type N< RET>. Then the labels for the 92123 zip code area appear, either on the screen or printer, depending on how you've answered the question about the printer. Why is this?

In the command file we've added the command ACCEPT ' Shall I send labels to the printer? (Y/N) ' TO YN which causes dBASE to present the question on the screen and wait for an answer. The answer is stored in a memory variable called YN. We've also added these lines to the command file.

```
IF !(YN)='Y'
        SET PRINT ON
ENDIF
```

These lines say "If the answer is Y, set the printer on." Notice the command actually checks to see if the uppercase equivalent is a Y. This is so that if we answered the question with a lowercase y, the printer would still be set on. Near the bottom of the command file, we've added the line

```
SET PRINT OFF
```

so that when the program was done printing labels, the printer was set back off automatically before returning to the dot prompt.

dBASE allows another method of decision making in command files called *macro substitution*.

```
********* Mailing Labels Program.
ERASE
ACCEPT ' What zip code area ' TO AREA

ACCEPT ' Shall I send labels to the printer? (Y/N) ' TO YN
IF !(YN)='Y'
     SET PRINT ON
ENDIF

GO TOP

DO WHILE .NOT. EOF
     IF ZIP = AREA
          ? TRIM(FNAME),LNAME
          ? ADDRESS
          ? TRIM(CITY)+', '+STATE+ZIP
          ?
          ?
          ?
     ENDIF
     SKIP
ENDDO
SET PRINT OFF
RETURN
```

Program 12.4

Macro Substitution

Macro substitution is a powerful programming technique used in command files. A macro is simply a memory variable name with an ampersand (&) in front of it. When dBASE encounters a macro in a command file, it replaces that macro with the contents of the memory variable. For example, if you have a memory variable called FLD, and you have the word ZIP stored to that name, every time the &FLD is encountered in the program, dBASE will automatically substitute the word ZIP.

Let's discuss a practical example. We've set up our labels program so that it asks for a zip code area to print labels for. However, we may actually want to print labels for a certain city or a certain state. We need to modify the command file so that it asks which field we wish to search on, and also what value to look for. That is, when we run the new version of the command file, we want it to ask

Search on which field?

and we can type in any field name (such as CITY, STATE, or ZIP). Then it will ask

Look for what _ ?

and we can type in a characteristic to search for. For example, if we answer the first question with the word CITY, the second question will appear as

Look for what CITY?

and we can type in a city. If we were to answer this question with Los Angeles, then only labels for Los Angeles residents would be printed. If we answered the first question with ZIP, the second question would ask "Search for what ZIP?" and we could type in a zip code to search for. This gives the command file more flexibility.

To allow this flexibility, we must modify the LABELS command file in Program 12.5 to include macros (the three new lines are shown in darker print).

Once we've changed the program, we can save the command file and then DO B:LABELS. When we do so, the screen clears and we see

Search on which field?

Let's answer by typing in City <RET>. Then the next question to appear is

Look for what City?

and we can answer by typing in San Diego <RET>. Then it asks

Shall I send labels to the printer? (Y/N):

We'll answer N <RET> for now, and then we see the mailing labels for the San Diego residents.

```
******** Mailing Labels Program.
ERASE

ACCEPT ' Search on which field? ' TO FLD
ACCEPT ' Look for what &FLD ' TO COND

ACCEPT ' Shall I send labels to the printer? (Y/N) ' TO YN
IF !(YN)='Y'
     SET PRINT ON
ENDIF

GO TOP

DO WHILE .NOT. EOF
   IF &FLD = '&COND'
        ? TRIM(FNAME),LNAME
        ? ADDRESS
        ? TRIM(CITY)+', '+STATE+ZIP
        ?
        ?
        ?
   ENDIF
   SKIP
ENDDO

SET PRINT OFF
RETURN
```

Program 12.5

John Q. Smith
123 A. St.
San Diego, CA 92123

Lucy Smithsonian
461 Adams St.
San Diego, CA 92122-1234

Let's try again. DO B:LABELS. The labels program asks

Search on which field?

and we type State < RET > . Then the command file asks

Look for what State?

and we type CA < RET > . It asks about the printer, to which we can reply Y or N, then prints mailing labels for all California residents. Let's discuss why. Near the top of the LABELS program, we see these two lines:

ACCEPT ' Search on which field? ' TO FLD
ACCEPT ' Look for what &FLD ' TO COND

When we run the program, the first line causes dBASE to display the question, "Search on which field?" and it waits for an answer. If we type in CITY < RET > in response to this question, dBASE stores the word CITY to a memory variable called FLD. Then the next line is executed, but it has a macro in it, &FLD. This causes the contents of the FLD variable to be substituted into this line, so what we see on the screen next is the question, "Look for what CITY?" Whatever we answer to this question gets stored to a memory variable called COND. Hence, if we answer this question with San Diego, we have two memory variables in RAM. One is called FLD, and it contains the word CITY. The other memory variable is called COND, and it contains the words San Diego. I could have named the memory variables anything I like, but I chose FLD and COND because they remind me of FIELD (to search on) and CONDition (to search for).

Then the command file asks about the printer, and begins the DO WHILE loop. Within the DO WHILE loop is the command IF &FLD = '&COND'. Before this line makes a decision to print a label or not, it is going to have to substitute in the macros. Hence, the line becomes IF CITY = 'San Diego', and only labels for San Diego residents are printed.

Had we answered the question "Search on which field?" with ZIP, and the question "Look for what ZIP?" with 92111, memory variable FLD would contain the word ZIP, and COND would contain 92111. In this case, when the program needed to make a decision as to whether or not to print a label, the IF statement would become IF ZIP = '92111'.

Macro substitution is a bit abstract, and takes a little getting used to. The only strict rule on macros is that they must be character-type memory variables.

Usually, when creating command files, we come up with an idea for a program we want, then we need to figure out just how to write the program. This is not too easy if you are a beginner. In the next chapter, we'll talk about methods that can help make the transition from an idea to a working program.

When we create a command file (program), we are actually *writing software*. There are four parts to writing software. First, we design the program by determining what it is to do for us. Second, we must write the program. In dBASE we do this by typing MODIFY COMMAND and then typing the program on the screen. Third, we run the program in order to test it. Fourth, since we often make mistakes when we first write the program, we need to make corrections to debug the program. Let's examine each of these steps in detail.

Step 1. The General Idea

It's a good idea to write down the general idea of a program on paper first. For example, let's say we want to develop a fancy mailing list system that's quick and easy to use. The general idea might read like this:

> This system will be designed to manage a mailing list, and will operate from a menu of choices. When first run, the system will display the Mail Menu as so:
>
> 1. Add new names and addresses.
> 2. Sort the mailing list.
> 3. Print names and addresses.
> 4. Edit data.
> 5. Exit the system.
>
> The option to print names and addresses will allow us to specify types of individuals to print data for. The system will be completely "menu-driven." That is, once we DO the main command file, jobs like adding new names, sorting, printing mailing labels, and editing will be performed by simply selecting menu options or answering questions on the screen. The system will be completely automated, so that an individual with no knowledge of dBASE II could still manage the mailing list.

Now that we have the general idea defined, we need to design a data base that will support it.

Step 2. Design the Data Base Structure

We'll structure the data base as follows:

#	FIELD NAME	TYPE	WIDTH	DECIMAL PLACES
1	LNAME	C	20	0
2	FNAME	C	15	0
3	ADDRESS	C	25	0
4	CITY	C	20	0
5	STATE	C	5	0
6	ZIP	C	10	0
7	PHONE	C	35	0

We've already created a data base with the structure, MAIL, so this step is done already.

Step 3. Develop Pseudocode

It's a little easier to write a program if we first write a reasonable facsimile of it in plain English. Doing so is called writing *pseudocode*. When we write pseudocode, we should try to specify the logic and series of events that will occur in the program, so that when we have to translate the program to actual dBASE language, much of the task is already defined. This isn't particularly easy, of course, because we're not accustomed to thinking like machines. But it's still easier to write a program from pseudocode jotted down on a piece of paper than from pure thought. Here's a pseudocoded example of the Mail Menu program for our mailing system:

COMMAND FILE NAME: MENU.CMD

PURPOSE: Present a menu of options for managing the mailing list.

PSEUDOCODE:

Set dBASE talk off
Use the mailing list data base
Set menu choice to 0

Repeat the Mail Menu until option to exit is selected
Clear the screen
Display the Mail Menu on the screen as follows:

Mail Menu

1. ADD new date

2. SORT data

3. PRINT data

4. EDIT data

5. EXIT the mailing system

Ask which option is desired

If option 1 selected
    Append new data

If option 2 selected
    Sort by last and first name

If option 3 selected
    Print mailing labels

If option 4 selected
    Edit data

Redisplay the Mail Menu (as long as option 5 was not selected)

Exit the mailing system

Notice that we've defined the logic of the MENU program here. We've also given it a title and mentioned its purpose. This is so that if it takes a long time to write the actual program, we can refer back to the pseudocode for reference. Notice that the pseudocode describes the task in English, but it looks like a program too. This intermediate step makes the next step a little easier. From this point, we'd need to write the actual program using proper dBASE II commands and syntax.

Step 4. Write the Program

Once we have a pseudocoded outline of the program, we need to write the actual program. In dBASE, we use MODIFY COMMAND for this. Let's now write the actual program. We cannot be as liberal with our sentences as we were in the pseudocode, because dBASE cannot understand English.
Let's

   MODIFY COMMAND B:MENU   < RET>

which brings us a blank screen to work with. Now we can type in the actual MENU program so that it looks like Program 13.1.
Now let's discuss how the actual program resembles the pseudocode above it. First, the command file sets the dBASE talk off, and uses B:MAIL as the data base. Then, it stores a zero to a memory variable called CHOICE. This is so that the DO WHILE CHOICE < 5

condition will be true when dBASE first enters the loop. Then it clears the screen and displays the Mail Menu using ? commands. Then it displays the question "Enter your choice (1–5) from above " and waits for an answer. Once an answer has been entered, the program performs the desired option. If the choice was 1, dBASE goes into APPEND mode. If the choice was 2, dBASE will sort by last name; if the choice was 3, dBASE will DO our other command file, B:LABELS, and so forth.

```
******************** Mailing List System Mail Menu

SET TALK OFF
USE B:MAIL
STORE 0 TO CHOICE

******************** Present mail Menu
DO WHILE CHOICE < 5
    ERASE
    ? '      Mail Menu'
    ?
    ? ' 1. Add new names'
    ? ' 2. Sort data'
    ? ' 3. Print Labels'
    ? ' 4. Edit data'
    ? ' 5. Exit the mailing system'
    ?
    INPUT ' Enter your choice (1-5) from above ' TO CHOICE

    ************* Perform appropriate task based on CHOICE

        IF CHOICE = 1
            APPEND
        ENDIF

        IF CHOICE = 2
            INDEX ON LNAME + FNAME TO B:NAMES
            USE B:MAIL INDEX B:NAMES
        ENDIF

        IF CHOICE = 3
            DO B:LABELS
        ENDIF

        IF CHOICE = 4
            EDIT
        ENDIF

ENDDO
```

Program 13.1

After the selected option has been performed, dBASE will eventually reach the ENDDO command at the bottom of the command file. The loop will repeat, redisplaying the Mail Menu and question. If the choice is 5 (exit) the DO WHILE CHOICE < 5 condition for the loop will cause the ENDDO not to repeat the loop, and the program will end.

Step 5. Run and Test the Program

Step 5 is not simply using the program, because as you probably know by now, we usually make a few mistakes in our program that need correcting. To test our program, of course, we still need to run it, so type in the command

    DO B:MENU   <RET>

After the screen is cleared, the Mail Menu is displayed.

Mail Menu

1. Add new names
2. Sort data
3. Print Data
4. Edit data
5. Exit the mailing system

Enter your choice (1–5) from above :

If we now type in 1 <RET>, dBASE will put us in the APPEND mode.

```
RECORD 00006
LNAME    :_              :
FNAME    :          :
ADDRESS :                    :
CITY     :          :
STATE    :      :
ZIP      :          :
PHONE    :                  :
```

So, anyone who typed in the command DO B:MENU could now add new data to the data base, even if they've never heard of the APPEND command. This is because the program has a line which states IF CHOICE = 1, and beneath that is the APPEND command. Since CHOICE did = 1, dBASE goes into APPEND mode. We can then add as many names to the mailing list as we wish. When we exit the APPEND mode (by pressing <RET> instead of typing in an LNAME), the Mail Menu reappears.

Mail Menu

1. Add new names

2. Sort data

3. Print Data

4. Edit data

5. Exit the mailing system

Enter your choice (1-5) from above :

Why? Because none of the IF clauses below the APPEND command in the program will be true. dBASE won't do the commands in IF CHOICE = 2 or IF CHOICE = 3, etc., because CHOICE = 1. When dBASE reaches the ENDDO command, CHOICE is less than 5, so the program loops around up to the DO WHILE CHOICE < 5 command, and the menu is redisplayed, and the INPUT question reappears. We could type in another option now, and whatever option we select (1–5) will be stored in CHOICE. Then, the appropriate function will take place (APPEND.INDEX, etc.).

Notice in the command file that if we select option #3, Print Labels, dBASE is told to DO a different command file, our LABELS progam. In this case, dBASE will DO B:LABELS. As you may recall, the last line in LABELS is the RETURN command. When one command file calls another (as in this case where MENU calls LABELS), the RETURN command tells dBASE to go back to where it left off in the first program. Therefore, MENU will DO B:LABELS, and LABELS will print the mailing labels and then RETURN to MENU.

I'm assuming here that your program ran right the first time. More likely, it didn't and you got one of dBASE's many error messages. We

usually don't see the errors in a program until we try to run the program. The computer catches them right away. The most common
errors that occur in command files are syntax errors, which result
from misspelling a command, a field name, or a variable name. Syntax errors also occur if we forget to put spaces between commands,
or if we attempt to use a field or memory variable that does not exist.

When dBASE encounters an error in a command file, it will display
an error message, and usually give us a chance to correct it. Let's take
a hypothetical example. Suppose when I had asked dBASE to DO
B:MENU, I got the message

```
* * * SYNTAX ERROR * * *
    ?
IF CHOCE = 1
CORRECT AND RETRY (Y/N)?
```

At first glance, we may not see the problem. But on close inspection,
we see that the word CHOICE is misspelled. dBASE attempted to find
a memory variable called CHOCE, and couldn't. If we answer Y to
the question CORRECT AND RETRY (Y/N), dBASE will ask

```
CHANGE FROM?
```

and we can type in CHOCE < RET>. Then dBASE will ask

```
CHANGE TO?
```

and we can type in the proper word, CHOICE < RET>. dBASE will
then show us the corrected line and ask if it needs more corrections:

```
IF CHOICE = 1
MORE CORRECTIONS (Y/N)?
```

Looks O.K., so we can answer N, and the program will continue on.

There is one catch though. When we make a correction in this fashion, it only makes the correction for the moment; it does not modify
the actual contents of the command file. To make the correction permanent, we'd need to edit the command file using the
MODIFY command as usual, make the change, and save with ^W.

Then we can DO the command file again, and that error will no longer occur. Others may occur, however, and we'll need to fix those in the same fashion. We often have to go through the test-and-debug cycle many times to get the program to run properly.

In the next chapter, we'll expand our mailing label system with more command files, and pick up some programming techniques in the process.

A MAILING LIST SYSTEM

14

In this chapter we'll be developing new programs to create a *menu-driven* mailing system. The term *menu-driven* means that the person using the programs we develop need only run one program. He simply selects options from a menu we develop in order to perform various tasks. Programmers create menu-driven systems so that individuals who don't know the commands of a language can still use the computer. The MENU command file we developed in the last chapter is such a program. In this chapter, we will expand the MENU command file to a complete mailing list management system.

The procedure again will be to describe, pseudocode, write, and test each new program. Then we'll link all the programs with our MENU program, so that we will have a complete menu-driven mailing list system. The programs have been fully tested and *debugged* (cleared of errors), so if you type one in and it doesn't work, you've probably typed something incorrectly. You will no doubt have to debug after you type these in, but your debugging will be limited to checking to see where you've failed to copy the contents of the command files exactly as they appear in the text.

Make sure you have the disk with MAIL.DBF in drive B, and you may want to SET TALK OFF before doing these.

The SORTER Command File

First we will develop a simple program (see Program 14.1) to allow for easy sorting. When we run sorter, the screen will clear and we'll see the following instructions on the screen:

How do you wish names sorted?
(Enter field name; LNAME, CITY, STATE, OR ZIP) :

When the sorting is complete, the program will inform us

SORT COMPLETE

Here is the pseudocode for SORTER.

PROGRAM   : SORTER.CMD

PURPOSE   : Allow for sort options to be displayed on the
              screen, then sort accordingly.

PSEUDOCODE :

Clear the screen
Display Instructions
Ask which field to sort on
Index accordingly
Return

To type in the command file, use the MODIFY command:

MODIFY COMMAND B:SORTER   < RET >

When the screen is ready, type in the command file exactly as it appears above. Save it with a ^W.
   Now let's

USE B:MAIL   < RET >
DO B:SORTER   < RET >

If you typed it in correctly, the screen will clear, then the instructions appear on the screen.

How do you wish names sorted?'
(Enter field name; LNAME, CITY, STATE, OR ZIP) :

Type in

LNAME   < RET >

then we see the message SORT COMPLETE, and the dot prompt. To test to see if it ran properly, just

LIST   < RET >

The records should now be sorted by last name.

```
*************** SORTER.CMD
ERASE
? ' How do you wish names sorted?'
ACCEPT '(Enter field name; LNAME, CITY, STATE, OR ZIP) ' TO FLD

INDEX ON &FLD TO B:MINDEX

?
? 'Sort complete'
RETURN
```

Program 14.1

00001	Appleby	Andy	345 Oak St.	Los Angeles	CA 92123
00004	Doe	Ruth	1142 J. St.	Los Angeles	CA 91234
00005	SMITH	Betsy	222 Lemon Dr.	New York	NY 01234
00002	Smith	John Q.	123 A. St.	San Diego	CA 92122
00003	Smithsonian	Lucy	461 Adams St.	San Diego	CA 92122-1234

If something went wrong, you'll have to use MODIFY COMMAND again to edit your program.

After we link sorter to the MENU program, it will sort, then return to the Mail Menu.

The EDDY Command File

At present, when we select the option to edit from the menu program, it asks us which record number to edit. It would be much easier to edit individuals by last name rather than record number. We'll design the EDDY command file to allow us to do this. This command file would be pseudocoded as follows:

PROGRAM: EDDY.CMD

PURPOSE: To allow editing by last name rather than record number.

PSEUDOCODE:

Clear the screen
Start a loop to keep asking for edits until no more edits are desired.

Within loop
  Clear screen
  Ask what name to edit

  Count how many people on the data base have that last name, and store count to a memory variable.

If nobody has that name
  Say 'there is no such person on the data base'
  Wait for response

If one person has that name
 Find that person
 Edit that record

If several people have that name
 List all people with that name
 Ask which one to edit

Ask if more names to edit
 If Yes, continue loop
Otherwise, return

The command file is shown in Program 14.2.

```
******************** Edit names and address (EDDY.CMD)
ERASE
SET EXACT ON
STORE 'Y' TO ANSWER

******************** Ask for names to edit while appropriate.
DO WHILE !(ANSWER) = 'Y'
   ERASE
   ACCEPT 'Edit whom? (Last name) ' TO WHOM
   COUNT FOR !(LNAME) = !(WHOM) TO WHOMS

   ************** If no such person, warn.
   IF WHOMS=0
      ?
      ? 'There is no &WHOM on the data base.'
   ENDIF

   ************** If 1 person with that name, edit.
   IF WHOMS=1
      LOCATE FOR LNAME=WHOM
      STORE # TO RECNO
      EDIT RECNO
   ENDIF

   ************** If more than 1 person with that last
   ************** name, display and get record number.
   IF WHOMS > 1
      ?
      LIST FOR !(LNAME)=!(WHOM) LNAME,FNAME,ADDRESS
      ?
      ACCEPT 'Which one (by record number) ' TO RECNO
      EDIT &RECNO
   ENDIF

   ************** Ask if more names to edit.
   ?
   ACCEPT ' Edit more names? (Y/N) ' TO ANSWER

ENDDO (while answer = 'Y')
SET EXACT OFF
RETURN
```

Program 14.2

In this program we use many of the commands we've already learned. Notice that we SET EXACT ON near the top of the program, so the searches will be exact rather than approximate. If one wishes to edit for Smith, there is no need to consider Smithsonians too. We SET EXACT OFF near the bottom of the program to return to the normal mode that dBASE uses (EXACT OFF). Also, when we COUNT or LIST FOR LNAME, we compare uppercase equivalents of each (!), so that we don't miss anyone whose name might have been inadvertently entered in all caps. This is a fairly large program, and may take some time to get typed in.

To enter and save the program, use the commands

    MODIFY COMMAND B:EDDY   <RET>

After the program is all typed in, save it with a ^W as usual. To run the program, type

    DO B:EDDY   <RET>

When it runs, we'll see

Edit whom? (Last name) :

Let's see what happens if we type in a name that we haven't listed on our mailing list.

    Jackson   <RET>

The program informs us that

There is no Jackson on the data base
Edit more names? (Y/N) :

Our program has told us that we've tried to edit someone who doesn't exist on the data file. It is also asking if we want to edit more names. Let's type in a Y <RET> and try one that we know is on the list. The screen is waiting with the question

Edit whom? (Last name) :

This time we'll respond with

    Appleby   <RET>

and we see on the screen:

```
RECORD 00001
LNAME     :Appleby              :
FNAME     :Andy         :
ADDRESS :345 Oak St.                   :
CITY        :Los Angeles    :
STATE      :CA   :
ZIP          :92123        :
PHONE    :                                          :
```

The program found Appleby for us, and put his data into the edit mode. We can move the cursor down to the ADDRESS field and change Andy's address to 123 A. St. Then move down and change his city to San Diego. Andy's record should look like this now:

```
RECORD 00001
LNAME     :Appleby              :
FNAME     :Andy         :
ADDRESS :123 A. St.                 :
CITY        :San Diego      :
STATE      :CA   :
ZIP          :92123        :
PHONE    :                                   :
```

When it does, type a ^W to save it. Now at the bottom of the screen, you should see the message

Edit more names? (Y/N) :

Let's try one more. Type in Y < RET >, so that the program again asks

Edit whom? (Last name) :

This time, type in

   Smith   < RET>

and we see on the screen:

```
00005   SMITH   Betsy      222 Lemon Dr.   New York    NY   01234
00002   Smith   John Q.    123 A. St.      San Diego   CA   92122
```

Which one (by record number) :

Since the program found two Smiths this time, it is asking which one we want to edit. Let's pick Betsy. Type in 5 <RET>, and we'll see

```
RECORD 00005
LNAME     :SMITH          :
FNAME     :Betsy      :
ADDRESS :222 Lemon Dr.            :
CITY      :New York       :
STATE     :NY    :
ZIP       :01234      :
PHONE   :                                    :
```

Let's delete her by typing a ^U. This displays

```
RECORD 00005 DELETED
LNAME     :SMITH      :
FNAME     :Betsy      :
ADDRESS :222 Lemon Dr.            :
CITY      :New York       :
STATE     :NY    :
ZIP       :01234      :
PHONE   :                                    :
```

Betsy is now marked for deletion. We could bring her back with another ^U, but for now let's leave her marked for deletion. Save her new data with a ^W now, and once again the program asks

Edit more names? (Y/N) :

Let's answer N <RET>, at which point the program ends and the dot prompt reappears.

The DELNAMES Command File

This program will automatically display records that have been marked for deletion, and give us a chance to recall any of them prior to packing the file. Here is the pseudocode:

PROGRAM: DELNAMES.CMD

PURPOSE: Display names marked for deletion, and allow for recalls, prior to packing the data base.

PSEUDOCODE:

Clear the screen
Set up a loop for recalling names
While recalling names
   Count how many records are marked for deletion

If no names are marked for deletion
   Display message 'no names to delete'
   Terminate loop

If names are marked for deletion
   Display names to be eliminated from the data base
   Ask if O.K. to eliminate all names
   If not O.K.
      Ask which to recall, and redisplay names to be eliminated
   If O.K.
      Pack the data base
Return

To enter the program, shown in Program 14.3, type

   MODIFY COMMAND B:DELNAMES <RET>

Once the program is typed in, save it. Then

   DO B:DELNAMES <RET>

which should bring up on the screen

00005 * SMITH   Betsy   222 Lemon Dr.   New York   NY   01234
Delete these individuals? (Y/N)

You can answer either Y or N. If you answer Y, the program will pack the data base, and Betsy will be eliminated. If we answer N, the program will ask

Keep which one? (by number) :

and we could unmark Betsy for deletion by simply typing in her record number, 5 <RET>. When we have decided whom we wish to delete, and whom we wish to recall, the program packs the data base and returns to the dot prompt.

```
**************** Before packing file, check.(DELNAMES.CMD)
ERASE
STORE 'N' TO PERMIT

DO WHILE !(PERMIT) = 'N'
    ERASE
    COUNT FOR * TO DELS

    ******************** If nothing to delete, don't bother.
    IF DELS = 0
        ?
        ? 'No names to delete'
        STORE 'Y' TO PERMIT
    ENDIF

    ******************** If many names to delete,
    ******************** display and get permission first.
    IF DELS > 0
        LIST FOR *
        ?
        ACCEPT 'Delete all these individuals? (Y/N) ' TO PERMIT
        IF !(PERMIT) = 'N'
            ACCEPT ' Keep which one (by number) ' TO RECNO
            RECALL RECORD &RECNO
        ENDIF (permit=n)
    ENDIF (dels > 0)
ENDDO (while permit = n)

PACK
RETURN
```

—Program 14.3—

The DUPES Command File

Every good computerized mailing system needs a built-in check-for-duplicates program. Mailing systems tend to grow, so they need to be trimmed down to avoid duplicate mailings. The DUPES.CMD command file checks the data base for identical street addresses in identical cities. When it finds duplicates, it tells us where they are so that we can view them through the EDIT command and decide whether or not to delete. It does not do any deleting itself, because in some cases we may want duplicates. For example, we may want to mail five items to the same address, because that address might be a large company with five individuals we wish to mail to.

Here is the pseudocode for the DUPES command file:

PROGRAM: DUPES.CMD

PURPOSE: Check for duplicate street addresses

PSEUDOCODE:

Clear the screen
Ask if duplicates should be sent to printer
If so, set printer on

Clear the screen
Index by address and city
Go to the top of the data base
Print report title (Duplicate street addresses)
Store 0 to counter of duplicate addresses

Set up loop to end of the data base
    Compare pairs of addresses by...
        Store top of pair to memory variable 1
        Store bottom of pair to memory variable 2
    If addresses match
        Display duplicate addresses
        Add 1 to counter of duplicate addresses
    Check next pair of addresses

When done
    If no duplicates found
        Display message 'No duplicates'
Return to dot prompt

In Program 14.4, you can see the entire program. Again, it is fairly lengthy and might take some time to type in. Use the command MODIFY COMMAND B:DUPES <RET> to create the program.

Once this command file is typed in and saved, we can run it with

DO B:DUPES   <RET>

The first thing it will ask is

Send duplicate addresses to printer? (Y/N) :

If you have a printer, you can answer Y <RET> if you like. Then the program will display all of the record numbers, addresses, and cities for which there are duplicate records. At this point, if you've followed along every step of the way, there are actually two duplicates on the data base, and this program will display them as

Duplicate Street Addresses

Record # 1 address is: 123 A. St. San Diego
Record # 2 address is: 123 A. St. San Diego

Press RETURN to return to Mail Menu :

At this point if we press RETURN, the dot prompt will appear. After we get all of these command files linked to the MENU program, the Mail Menu will appear.

Linking the Command Files to the Mail Menu

Now we can link all of our command files together, so that all we have to do to use the mailing system is type in the command DO MENU, and select options from the Mail Menu displayed below.

Mail Menu
1. Add new names
2. Sort data
3. Print Labels
4. Edit data
5. Pack the data base
6. Check for duplicates
7. Exit the mailing system
Enter your choice (1–7) from above :

```
*************** Check for duplicate addresses  (DUPES.CMD)

ERASE
******************************* This routine checks for duplicate
******************************* street addresses by indexing on
******************************* addresss, then checking to see if
******************************* pairs of addresses match.

ACCEPT ' Send duplicate addresses to printer? (Y/N) ' TO YN

IF !(YN)='Y'
   SET PRINT ON
ENDIF


ERASE

*************************** Create an index of street addresses

INDEX ON ADDRESS + CITY TO B:STREETS
GO TOP
*************************** Now, starting at the top of the file,
*************************** check to see if the address we're
*************************** "looking at" is identical to the address
*************************** directly underneath.
?
? '   Duplicate Street Addresses'
?
?
STORE 0 TO COUNTER
DO WHILE .NOT. EOF
   STORE ADDRESS+CITY TO AD1
   SKIP 1
   IF .NOT. EOF
      STORE ADDRESS+CITY TO AD2
   ENDIF

   ****** Compare the two addresses (upper case for accuracy)
   ****** If they match, print on report

   IF !(AD1)=!(AD2)
      SKIP -1
      ? ' Record # ' + STR(#,4) + ' address is: ',TRIM(ADDRESS),CITY
      SKIP 1
      ? ' Record # ' + STR(#,4) + ' address is: ',TRIM(ADDRESS),CITY
      ?
   STORE COUNTER + 1 TO COUNTER
   ENDIF
   STORE ' ' TO AD2
ENDDO  (While end of file has not been reached)

************* If none found, display message.
IF COUNTER = 0
   ? ' No Duplicates Found'
ENDIF

************* Pause, then return to Mail Menu.
?
?
ACCEPT ' Press RETURN to return to Mail Menu ' TO NOTHING

USE B:MAIL
RETURN
```

Program 14.4

We can choose whatever option we wish and the mailing system will perform accordingly. When we are done with the particular option we selected, the menu will reappear on the screen. We can keep selecting options as long as we wish. When we're done selecting, option #7 will return us to the dot prompt.

To link all of the command files into one integrated menu-driven mailing list system now requires that we modify MENU.CMD so that it calls up the various command files. Here is how MENU.CMD must look in order to provide links to these command files. The new or modified lines are in darker print in Program 14.5.

```
****************** Mailing List System Mail Menu

SET TALK OFF
USE B:MAIL
STORE 0 TO CHOICE

********************** Present mail Menu
DO WHILE CHOICE < 7
         ? '      Mail Menu'
         ?
         ? '  1. Add new names'
         ? '  2. Sort data'
         ? '  3. Print Labels'
         ? '  4. Edit data'
         ? '  5. Pack the data base'
         ? '  6. Check for duplicates'
         ? '  7. Exit the mailing system'
         ?
INPUT ' Enter your choice (1-7) from above ' TO CHOICE

************ Perform appropriate task based on CHOICE

       IF CHOICE = 1
           APPEND
       ENDIF

       IF CHOICE = 2
           DO B:SORTER
       ENDIF

       IF CHOICE = 3
           DO B:LABELS
       ENDIF

       IF CHOICE = 4
             DO B:EDDY
       ENDIF

       IF CHOICE = 5
              DO B:DELNAMES
       ENDIF

       IF CHOICE = 6
            DO B:DUPES
       ENDIF
ENDDO (while choice < 7)
```

Program 14.5

Once you type in and use the mailing list system for a while, you'll probably find room for new features or improvements. By all means, try writing your own command files. Mailing list programs are a good place to start learning some programming techniques. Run the programs in this book, then study them to see how they perform their tasks. In many ways, learning to program is learning to use other peoples' programming techniques.

When you start creating your own command files, the debugging process becomes more involved. Many beginning programmers are hampered by not knowing what to do when their program doesn't work quite as they expected. In the next chapter, we'll discuss debugging techniques.

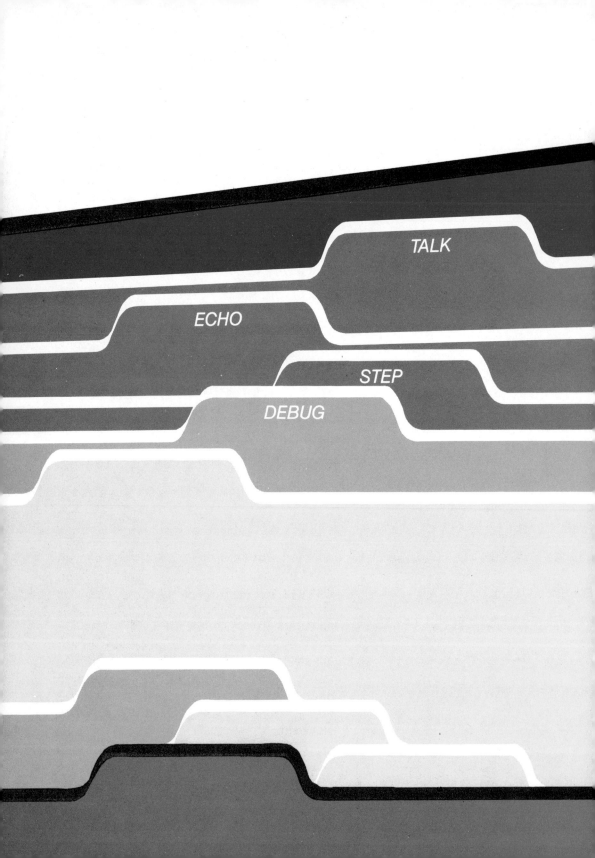

DEBUGGING TECHNIQUES

15

When our programs fail to perform as expected, we often stare at the screen helplessly and think, "Now what do I do?" Some errors are fairly obvious and easy to fix, such as when we misspelled CHOICE in the last chapter. Sometimes, however, dBASE will display a line as having an error in it, and we don't see the error. At that point, we may need to go deeper into our search for the error. Here are some good techniques that can help.

DISPLAY MEMORY and DISPLAY STRUCTURE

One of the best techniques for debugging a command file is to display the contents of memory variables in RAM shortly after the error occurs. An error usually causes dBASE to ask if we wish to CORRECT AND RETRY? If we answer <ESC> to this question, dBASE returns to the dot prompt. From there, we can DISPLAY MEMORY and look for suspicious data in memory variables. Make sure memory variables are of the exact type you intended. Most errors are caused by treating numbers as character strings or vice versa. Watch out for those. Also, check for valid data stored in memory variables. If something looks suspicious, go back to the command file and see if you can determine what went wrong.

dBASE will produce a SYNTAX ERROR if we attempt to print the contents of a field or a memory variable that does not exist. For instance, if we attempt to '? ADRESS', we might get a SYNTAX ERROR, because the field ADRESS does not exist. Perhaps the field ADDRESS exists, but ADRESS does not. If we DISPLAY MEMORY variables, we can see if the memory variable exists. If it does not, we can check to see if it exists as a field by using the DISPLAY STRUC-TURE command. Misspelled commands and improper ordering of words in a statement will also cause SYNTAX ERRORS.

SET TALK ON

In the mailing list system command file, we SET TALK OFF at the top of the Mail Menu program. If we eliminate this line from the command file, and SET TALK ON before we DO the command file, dBASE's extraneous messages will be displayed on the screen. These extraneous messages can be useful to us for watching events as they occur in the command file. They may lead to clues to errors in our program.

SET ECHO ON

An exaggerated version of SET TALK ON is the SET ECHO ON command. This displays every command line in the dBASE program as it is being processed. Thus, we can see everything that the command file is doing as it is running. It goes by pretty fast, but we can slow it down considerably with SET STEP ON.

SET STEP ON

If you want to follow the logic of your command file as it is running, step by step, leave ECHO on, and SET STEP ON. Your command file will be processed one line at a time. As each line is processed, you can pause, continue, or stop processing. This is great for those hard-to-find little bugs that hide in tiny dark logical crevices.

SET DEBUG ON

The option to SET DEBUG ON can also be very helpful for getting at the hard-to-find errors. When the DEBUG parameter is on, all the outputs from SET ECHO ON and/or SET STEP ON are sent directly to the printer and are not displayed on the screen. Hence we can watch our command perform on the screen without distraction from the ECHO command. On the printer, the actual lines within the command file will appear as dBASE is doing them, as well as the results of each line. We can then study the hardcopy of the events that occured in the program. If other attempts failed, this will usually lead us to the source of the problem.

Make a Hardcopy of the Program

The next thing to do is get a copy of your command file to the printer. If you have word processing software (like the WordStar program), just make a listing as you would for any other document (but always use nondocument mode for editing command files). If you use the CP/M™ operating system, you can use the PIP command to get a quick hardcopy of your command file. This requires that your CP/M disk be in drive A, and your command file be on drive B (or some other drive, but readily accessible). With the CP/M A> showing on the screen, type

    PIP LST: = B:filenam.CMD[P]

and your command file will be sent to the printer with page breaks. The filename above refers to the name of the file you wish to print (e.g., PIP LST: = B:MENU.CMD).

If you're using MS-DOS or PC-DOS, you can send command files to the printer using the TYPE command. First, hold down the CTRL key and press the P key. Then type in the command TYPE FILE-NAME.PRG. After the command file is listed on the printer, press ^P again to disconnect from the printer. (Note: for MS-DOS and PC-DOS systems press the ^PrtSc key.)

When you get a hardcopy, draw arrows from your DO WHILEs and their respective ENDDOs. Likewise for IF...ENDIF clauses. You may find dangling DO WHILEs that don't have ENDDOs associated with them, or IFs and ENDIFs which are crossed over and are throwing everything out of whack. In Program 15.1 is a printed command file with the DO...ENDDOs attached. Notice that they all match up, and that none of the arrows cross over one another.

It is easiest to do this working from the smaller, innermost DO loops and IF clauses to the larger, outermost loops and IF clauses. After you mark your routines in this way, study the program again in this light. You may find errors in your logic based on the arrows themselves.

```
    ******************** Count to 5, 10 times.
    STORE 1 TO OUTLOOP
    STORE 1 TO INLOOP

    ******** Do outer-most loop 10 times
  ┌─DO WHILE OUTLOOP < 11
    ? 'OUTER LOOP NUMBER : ' + STR(OUTLOOP,2)

        ************* For each outer loop, do 5 inner loops
  │ ┌──►DO WHILE INLOOP < 6
  │ │     ? INLOOP
  │ │     STORE INLOOP + 1 TO INLOOP
  │ └──►ENDDO (while inloop < 6)

    STORE 1 TO INLOOP
    STORE OUTLOOP + 1 TO OUTLOOP
  └─►ENDDO (while ouloop < 11)
```

└─*Program 15.1*─────

Let's try out some debugging aids with a sample program which includes some errors. Using the command

> MODIFY COMMAND B:TEST   <RET>

we can create and save the command file in Program 15.2. Now when we

> DO B:TEST   <RET>

we simply get another dot prompt. Yet, we know there should have been some labels printed. In order to catch the errors, we can watch the flow of the program by using the command

> SET ECHO ON   <RET>

Then once again we'll

> DO B:TEST   <RET>

Now we can see each line being processed as dBASE does the command file. On the screen we'll see:

USE B:MAIL
DO WHILE NOT EOF

Hmmm. It looks like the command file only got as far as the DO WHILE line in the command file. We can watch each individual line

```
*************************************************
* TEST.CMD                                      *
*************************************************
SET TALK OFF
USE B:MAIL

DO WHILE NOT EOF
   IF ZIP = '92122'
      ? TRIM(FNAME), LANME
      ? ADDRESS
      ? TRIM(CITY)+', '+STATE+ ZIP
      ?
      ?
      ?
   ENDIF
SKIP
ENDDO
```

Program 15.2

being processed, one step at a time, by typing in the command:

SET STEP ON   <RET>

Now when we

DO B:TEST   <RET>

we see

SINGLE STEP   Y: = STEP,   N: = KEYBOARD CMD,   ESC: = CANCEL Y
SINGLE STEP   Y: = STEP,   N: = KEYBOARD CMD,   ESC: = CANCEL Y
SINGLE STEP   Y: = STEP,   N: = KEYBOARD CMD,   ESC: = CANCEL Y
SINGLE STEP   Y: = STEP,   N: = KEYBOARD CMD,   ESC: = CANCEL Y
USE B:MAIL
SINGLE STEP   Y: = STEP,   N: = KEYBOARD CMD,   ESC: = CANCEL Y
SINGLE STEP   Y: = STEP,   N: = KEYBOARD CMD,   ESC: = CANCEL Y
DO WHILE NOT EOF
SINGLE STEP   Y: = STEP,   N: = KEYBOARD CMD,   ESC: = CANCEL Y
SINGLE STEP   Y: = STEP,   N: = KEYBOARD CMD,   ESC: = CANCEL Y

There are several blank lines in the program, so there are many single steps. Notice we've answered each step with a Y to move to the next line. Still, the program only gets as far as the DO WHILE command. Looking at it more closely, we can now see the problem: we've forgotten to put the periods around the NOT operator (.NOT.). So now we

MODIFY COMMAND B:TEST   <RET>

and correct the error by making TEST look like Program 15.3.

Now we can save the edited command file (^W), then set the debugging parameters off when the dot prompt reappears. That is, we'll

SET ECHO OFF   <RET>
SET STEP OFF   <RET>

Now we'll

DO B:TEST   <RET>

and we find another error:

```
* * * SYNTAX ERROR * * *
    ? TRIM (FNAME),LANME
CORRECT AND RETRY (Y/N?   <ESC>
```

We can press the escape key in response to the question CORRECT AND RETRY? which brings back the dot prompt. Notice the question mark before the field name LANME. We should check to see if such a field or memory variable exists. First, we can check the memory variables with the command

DISPLAY MEMORY   <RET>

and we see

* * TOTAL * *   00 VARIABLES USED 00000 BYTES USED

no memory variables. Now we can check the data base structure to see what fields exist using the command

DISPLAY STRUCTURE   <RET>

```
**************************************************
* TEST.CMD                                       *
**************************************************
SET TALK OFF
USE B:MAIL

DO WHILE .NOT. EOF
   IF ZIP = '92122'
       ? TRIM(FNAME), LANME
       ? ADDRESS
       ? TRIM(CITY)+', '+STATE+ ZIP
       ?
       ?
       ?
    ENDIF
  SKIP
  ENDDO
```

Program 15.3

and we see:

STRUCTURE FOR FILE: B:MAIL.DBF

NUMBER OF RECORDS: 00008

DATE OF LAST UPDATE: 00/00/00

PRIMARY USE DATABASE

FLD	NAME	TYPE	WIDTH	DEC
001	LNAME	C	015	
002	FNAME	C	020	
003	COMPANY	C	015	
004	ADDRESS	C	020	
005	CITY	C	015	
006	STATE	C	005	
007	ZIP	C	008	
008	PHONE	C	035	
009	KEYWORDS	C	080	

* * TOTAL * *

There is a field named LNAME, but not one called LANME. Obviously we've misspelled the field name in our command file. So once again we have to

    MODIFY COMMAND B:TEST   <RET>

and correct the spelling of LANME so the TEST.CMD now looks like Program 15.4.

```
****************************************************
* TEST.CMD                                         *
****************************************************
SET TALK OFF
USE B:MAIL

DO WHILE .NOT. EOF
    IF ZIP = '92122'
        ? TRIM(FNAME), LNAME
        ? ADDRESS
        ? TRIM(CITY)+', '+STATE+ ZIP
        ?
        ?
        ?
    ENDIF
    SKIP
ENDDO
```

Program 15.4

Now when we

```
DO B:TEST   <RET>
```

we'll see mailing labels for individuals in the 92122 zip code area because the program doesn't have any more bugs. Here is our list:

John Q. Smith
123 A. St.
San Diego, CA 92122

Lucy Smithsonian
461 Adams St.
San Diego, CA 92122

Unfortunately, debugging isn't always this simple. Learning to become a good troubleshooter takes as much experience as learning to be a good programmer.

To summarize, the most common programming errors to watch out for are:

- Confusing character strings and numbers.

- Dangling DO WHILEs and ENDIFs. Also, crossed loops and IF clauses, which cause an ENDIF to respond to the wrong IF, or an ENDDO to respond to the wrong DO WHILE.

- Putting a command line in an IF...ENDIF clause that actually belongs outside the clause. This is a very common error which can wreak havoc on the program's results. Likewise, putting a command line inside a loop which belongs outside the loop. This can cause infinite loops to occur. Along this same line, forgetting to SKIP inside a 'DO WHILE .NOT. EOF' loop will cause an infinite loop to occur, because the loop will just keep rereading the first record over and over again.

- Misspelling a command, memory variable name, or field name. If we create a field called ADDRESS, and later attempt to ? ADRESS or INDEX ON ADRESS, an error is sure to occur. We called the field ADDRESS, and we're telling dBASE to look for ADRESS, which does not exist.

- Not bothering with design or pseudocode. When we come up with a good idea for a new program, we're tempted to just start typing it into the computer, and make it up as we go along. This can lead to a tangled mess of commands in a program that is very difficult to untangle later. A little preplanning can save a lot of confusion.

Now let me give you a little pep talk on debugging. All programs have bugs. They are big ones at first, which eventually get refined down to very small ones. Even software systems that have been in use for a while (like dBASE II) have bugs in them. The professional does not take his bugs to heart. He does not sulk or pout over them, nor does he shake his fist at the CRT's blank stare (at least, not while anyone is looking). He knows that the computer can't do what he *means*, and so he is going to have to spell it out more clearly. The beginner, on the other hand, often feels intimidated, frustrated, or angered by his software bugs. This is not good. One should not get one's ego involved with one's software (at least, not until it's debugged and running).

The most important skill to develop in writing software is to break down big complex problems into smaller, workable pieces. The second most important skill is to say exactly what you mean, using the computer's extremely limited vocabulary. Experience helps us develop these skills. It's actually the debugging experience which best helps us learn to express ourselves in computer language.

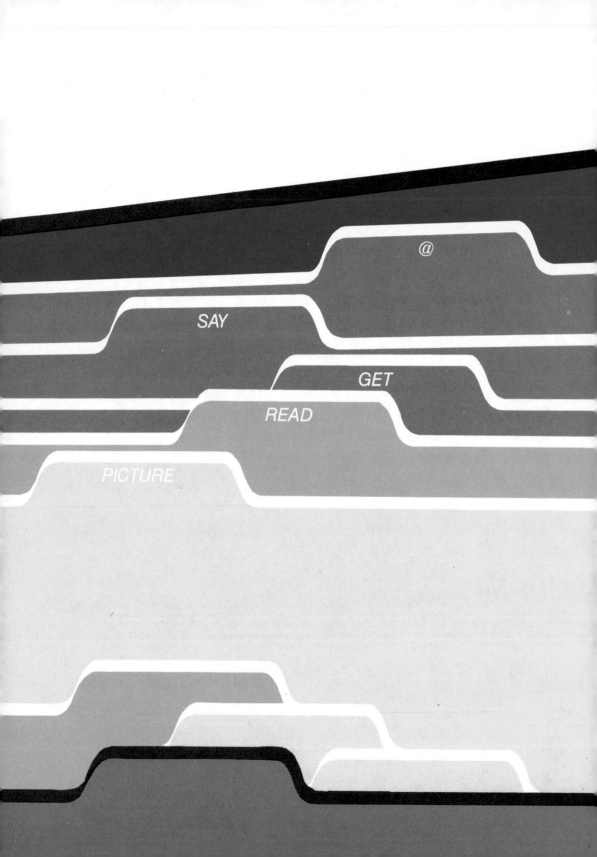

SETTING UP SCREEN DISPLAYS

16

dBASE automatically provides us with many forms to fill out for adding or editing data. For example, when we USE B:MAIL and APPEND, we get the append form on the screen.

The append form is shown in the screen below.

```
RECORD 00006
LNAME    :_                 :
FNAME    :           :
ADDRESS :                          :
CITY     :            :
STATE    :    :
ZIP      :          :
PHONE    :            :
```

In addition to these ready-made forms, dBASE allows us to create our own forms. For example, we might want to enter mail data using a form like this:

```
Record Number 6
Enter  ^W as last name to quit.


Last Name :                : First Name :            :
Address :                         :
City :             : State :    : Zip :            :
Phone :            :
```

This form is better than the first one because it provides instructions such as "Enter ^W as last name to quit," and it has the field names spelled out (Last Name instead of LNAME). To create such forms of our own, we need to use the @, SAY, GET, and READ commands.

Creating Forms with @, SAY, GET, and READ

The @ command tells dBASE where on the screen to position the cursor prior to printing something. It works by row and column number (@ ROW,COLUMN) where rows and columns are numbers. The upper left corner of the screen is row 0, column 0. The lower left corner is row 23 (on most screens), column 0. The upper right corner is row 0, column 80, and the lower right corner is row 23, column 80. The SAY command tells dBASE what to print at the cursor postion (SAY 'some message'). Hence, next to the dBASE dot prompt, if we were to type in the command

   @ 12,40 SAY 'Hi'   <RET>

we'd see the word "Hi" printed near the middle of the screen.

The GET command tells dBASE what information dBASE is to get from the screen (GET field name) when a READ command is encountered in the command file. To illustrate this, let's create a command file called ADDNAMES. That is, let's

   MODIFY COMMAND B:ADDNAMES   <RET>

and type in the command file in Program 16.1. If we save the command file, then

   DO B:ADDNAMES   <RET>

we see on the screen

Record Number 6
Enter ^W as last name to quit.

Last Name :_   : First Name :   :
Address :   :
City :   : State :   : Zip :   :
Phone :   :

```
        ********* Program to set up screen display for adding new data.
        USE B:MAIL
        ERASE
        APPEND BLANK
        ? 'Record number ',#
        ? 'Enter ^W as last name to quit.'

        @ 4,1 SAY 'Last Name ' GET LNAME
        @ 4,35 SAY 'First Name ' GET FNAME
        @ 5,1 SAY 'Address ' GET ADDRESS
        @ 6,1 SAY 'City ' GET CITY
        @ 6,27 SAY 'State ' GET STATE
        @ 6,40 SAY 'Zip ' GET ZIP
        @ 7,1 SAY 'Phone ' GET PHONE
        READ
```
Program 16.1

We can type in the information just as we would using the APPEND command. Notice that the cursor is positioned at the beginning of the last name field (the first GET field). We can type in a last name, press the return key, and the cursor goes to the beginning of the first name field, and waits for us to type in a first name. We can use the usual cursor control commands to move the cursor around inside the form should we need to correct errors. Let's fill in the form to add Dusty Rhodes to our mail data base.

```
Record Number 6

Enter ^W as last name to quit.


Last Name :Rhodes            : First Name :Dusty        :
Address :P.O. Box 1234       :
City :Los Angeles   : State :CA    : Zip :91234         :
Phone :(213) 555-1212               :
```

After we fill in the phone number and press RETURN, we'll be returned to the dot prompt. If we then

    LIST   <RET>

we see her information has been added.

```
00001  Appleby       Andy      123 A. St.     San Diego    CA  92123

00002  Smith         John Q.   123 A. St.     San Diego    CA  92122

00003  Smithsonian   Lucy      461 Adams St.  San Diego    CA  92122-1234

00004  Doe           Ruth      1142 J. St.    Los Angeles  CA  91234

00005  SMITH         Betsy     222 Lemon Dr.  New York     NY  01234

00006  Rhodes        Dusty     P.O. Box 12345 Los Angeles  CA  91234

       (213) 555-1212
```

Let's discuss why.
    The first two lines of the command file tell dBASE to USE B:MAIL then clear the screen (ERASE). The next line (APPEND BLANK) tells dBASE to append a blank record (APPEND BLANK) to the bottom of the MAIL data base. At this point, MAIL will have a new record on it, but all the fields will contain blanks. The next two lines tell dBASE to

print a couple of simple messages on the screen, "Record Number" (with # displayed), and an instruction to "Enter a CTRL-W as last name to quit."

The next seven lines tell dBASE how to display our form on the screen. dBASE is told to display the message "Last Name" at row 4, column 1; at row 4, column 35, to display the message "First Name," and so forth. dBASE displays each of the SAY messages until it reaches the READ command at the bottom of the command file. As soon as dBASE encounters the READ command, it positions the cursor inside the first GET statement on the screen (GET LNAME). dBASE then waits for something to be typed on the screen. Whatever is typed in becomes LNAME for the new record. Then the READ command causes the cursor to jump to the next GET field (FNAME), and dBASE again waits for some data to be typed in.

This procedure continues until all of the GET fields have had some data typed in. At that point, dBASE is done reading; the program ends, and the dot prompt appears.

In our practice example, we did a LIST after filling out the form to see that dBASE had indeed appended the new data to the data base. That is, it first appended a new record with all blank fields (APPEND BLANK), then it replaced the blank fields in that record with the information typed in on the form.

We can make our forms a little fancier still by using templates.

Making Templates with PICTURE

The PICTURE command can be used with @, SAY, and GET to provide templates on the screen. For example, suppose we want our form to look like this:

Record Number 6
Enter ^W as last name to quit.

Last Name :_   : First Name :   :
Address :   :
City :   : State :   : Zip :   :
Phone :(   )   -   :

Notice that the PHONE field has a template embedded in it that resembles a typical phone number format :( ) - :. The PICTURE command allows us to set up such a template, and also to limit the types of data that are acceptable for a given field. Here are some of the PICTURE data types:

Format Character	Acceptable Data
# or 9	Accepts only numeric digits (1,2,3...8,9,0) and +, −, and blanks.
A	Accepts only alphabetical characters (A–Z).
X	Accepts any data.

Let's try out an example. Let's MODIFY COMMAND B:ADDNAMES to look like Program 16.2. Notice the only change is in the line which reads @ 7,1 SAY PHONE. We've added PICTURE '(999) 999-9999'. Now when we save the command file and DO B:ADDNAMES we see

Record Number 7
Enter ^W as last name to quit.

Last Name :_   : First Name :   :
Address :   :
City :   : State :   : Zip :   :
Phone :( )   -   :

```
     ******** Program to set up screen display for adding new data.
     USE B:MAIL
     ERASE
     APPEND BLANK
     ? 'Record number ',#
     ? 'Enter ^W as last name to quit.'

     @ 4,1 SAY 'Last Name ' GET LNAME
     @ 4,35 SAY 'First Name ' GET FNAME
     @ 5,1 SAY 'Address ' GET ADDRESS
     @ 6,1 SAY 'City ' GET CITY
     @ 6,27 SAY 'State ' GET STATE
     @ 6,40 SAY 'Zip ' GET ZIP
     @ 7,1 SAY 'Phone ' GET PHONE PICTURE '(999)999-9999'
     READ
```
Program 16.2

Fill out the form as below. When you type in the phone number, try typing in some alphabetical characters first. dBASE will beep and refuse to accept them, because the PICTURE format specifies numbers only.

Record Number 7

Enter ^W as last name to quit.

Last Name :Frisbee   : First Name :Hobart   :

Address :321 Third Ave.   :

City :Cucamonga   : State :CA   : Zip :91234   :

Phone :(213) 555-0101:

After all the data are typed in, the dot prompt reappears. If we now

    LIST   <RET>

we see

00001	Appleby	Andy	123 A. St.	San Diego	CA	92123
00002	Smith	John Q.	123 A. St.	San Diego	CA	92122
00003	Smithsonian	Lucy	461 Adams St.	San Diego	CA	92122-1234
00004	Doe	Ruth	1142 J. St.	Los Angeles	CA	91234
00005	SMITH	Betsy	222 Lemon Dr.	New York	NY	01234
00006	Rhodes	Dusty	P.O. Box 12345	Los Angeles	CA	91234
	(213) 555-1212					
00007	Frisbee	Hobart	321 Third Ave.	Cucamonga	CA	91234
	(213) 555-0101					

Notice that Hobart's phone number contains parentheses and a hyphen, even though we did not type these on the screen when we entered the phone number. This is because the PICTURE template specified that these characters are part of the field. When we have a great deal of data to enter, these templates can save us some repetitive typing.

Looping through the Entry Screen

Our ADDNAMES command file has one strong disadvantage. It only allows us to enter one record, then it returns to the dot prompt. Ideally, we'd like it to keep asking for names and addresses until we're done, like the APPEND command does. To give ADDNAMES this capability, we're going to have to insert a loop. Let's set up a loop in ADDNAMES with two new lines, DO WHILE and ENDDO as shown in Program 16.3. The existing lines are indented inside the loop for readability, but this is not necessary.

If we now save the new ADDNAMES command file and then use the command DO, we see on the screen

Record Number 8
Enter ^W as last name to quit.

Last Name :_   : First Name :   :
Address :   :
City :   : State :   : Zip :   :
Phone :(   )   -   :

and we can fill in whatever data we wish. Let's add May Johnson.

```
     ******** Program to set up screen display for adding new data.
     USE B:MAIL

     DO WHILE LNAME # ' ' .OR. # = 0
         ERASE
         APPEND BLANK
         ? 'Record number ',#
         ? 'Enter ^W as last name to quit.'

         @ 4,1 SAY 'Last Name ' GET LNAME
         @ 4,35 SAY 'First Name ' GET FNAME
         @ 5,1 Say 'Address ' GET ADDRESS
         @ 6,1 SAY 'City ' GET CITY
         @ 6,27 SAY 'State ' GET STATE
         @ 6,40 SAY 'Zip ' GET ZIP
         @ 7,1 SAY 'Phone ' GET PHONE PICTURE '(999)999-9999'
         READ
     ENDDO
```

—Program 16.3—

Record Number 8
Enter ^W as last name to quit.

Last Name :Johnson   : First Name :May   :
Address :123 Oak St.   :
City :Boston   : State :MA   : Zip :01234   :
Phone :(111) 111-1111:

As soon as we're done, an empty format is displayed:

Record Number 9
Enter ^W as last name to quit.

Last Name :_   : First Name :   :
Address :   :
City :   : State :   : Zip :   :
Phone :(   )   -   :

Now dBASE is asking for data on record 9. We can choose to fill in more data, or we can type a ^W to get the dot prompt again. Let's analyze the logic of the command file in more detail.

The command file starts out by using B:MAIL. At that instant, dBASE is positioned to the first record in the MAIL data base, and the first name on the data base is Appleby (LNAME='Appleby'). Then, dBASE decides whether or not to do all the commands inside the loop. Well, LNAME='Appleby', not ' ', so dBASE will proceed through the loop (DO WHILE LNAME # ' '). (.OR. # = 0 is explained below.)

Inside the loop, dBASE appends a blank record, displays the formatted screen, and reads the data from the screen as we type them in. Then, the ENDDO command causes dBASE to jump back to the DO WHILE command, because LNAME now = 'Johnson', (not ' '). dBASE appends another blank record, and asks for its data. If we enter ^W instead of a last name, the READ command responds by skipping all further GET commands. dBASE is then at the ENDDO command again. Now, LNAME = ' ' because we did not type in a last name. So dBASE does not repeat the loop (Do while LNAME does NOT = a blank). The program ends and the dot prompt appears.

I put in the additional looping condition, .OR. #=0, (.OR. record number equals zero) not because it was necessary in this particular instance, but because in a more general sense it is needed. Had the MAIL data base been empty, the loop would not function. Here is why. The first line in the command file would use MAIL, and discover that it contained zero records. At that point, LNAME = ' ' (no last name). Hence, the DO WHILE LNAME # ' ' loop would not work, because LNAME *DOES* = ' '. So, I made the DO WHILE loop occur under two conditions: 1) last names are still being added, or 2) it's a brand new data base without any records in it. Keep this in mind when you start creating your own data entry routines; it might save you some headaches.

Unfortunately, we're not quite done. There is still one more catch. If we were to

LIST   <RET>

we'd see

00001	Appleby	Andy	123 A. St.	San Diego	CA	92123
00002	Smith	John Q.	123 A. St.	San Diego	CA	92122
00003	Smithsonian	Lucy	461 Adams St.	San Diego	CA	92122-1234
00004	Doe	Ruth	1142 J. St.	Los Angeles	CA	91234
00005	SMITH	Betsy	222 Lemon Dr.	New York	NY	01234
00006	Rhodes	Dusty	P.O. Box 12345	Los Angeles	CA	91234
	(213) 555-1212					
00007	Frisbee	Hobart	321 Third Ave.	Cucamonga	CA	91234
	(213) 555-0101					
00008	Johnson	May	123 Oak St.	Boston	MA	01234
	(111) 111-1111					
00009						

Notice that there is a blank at record 9, at the bottom of the data base. This is because the command file appends a blank record prior to asking for LNAME. When we type in ^W to quit adding names, record 9 stays in the data base with all blank fields. Unfortunately, every time we add new names, we add another blank record to the end of the data base. These blank records waste space and confuse things. The solution to this problem is to have the command file automatically delete the last (blank) record prior to ending. We can add a few lines to the bottom of the command file as in Program 16.4. Now dBASE will delete and pack the blank record from the bottom of the data base before returning to the dot prompt. Note: The PACK command is optional in this program. If you choose to leave it out, the bottom record will just be marked for deletion, and you can pack the data base at a later time if you wish.

Linking the ADDNAMES Program to the MENU Program

I've added the RETURN command to the end of ADDNAMES so we can link ADDNAMES to our MENU command file like the other

```
******** Program to set up screen display for adding new data.
USE B:MAIL

DO WHILE LNAME # ' ' .OR. # = 0
    ERASE
    APPEND BLANK
    ? 'Record number ',#
    ? 'Enter ^W as last name to quit.'

    @ 4,1 SAY 'Last Name ' GET LNAME
    @ 4,35 SAY 'First Name ' GET FNAME
    @ 5,1 Say 'Address ' GET ADDRESS
    @ 6,1 SAY 'City ' GET CITY
    @ 6,27 SAY 'State ' GET STATE
    @ 6,40 SAY 'Zip ' GET ZIP
    @ 7,1 SAY 'Phone ' GET PHONE PICTURE '(999)999-9999'
    READ
ENDDO

********************* Delete bottom (blank) record.
GO BOTTOM
DELETE
PACK
RETURN
```

Program 16.4

command files we've created. To do so, we need to MODIFY COM-
MAND B:MENU, so that the IF clause which reads

```
IF  CHOICE  =1
        APPEND
ENDIF
```

looks like this:

```
IF  CHOICE  =1
        DO  B:ADDNAMES
ENDIF
```

Then, when we DO B:MENU, our Mail Menu of choices is displayed. If we select option #1 (add new names), the ADDNAMES
command file takes over the job of adding new names to the data
base. When we enter a ^W to quit adding names, the Mail Menu is
redisplayed on the screen.

SOME USEFUL TIPS

17

Before ending this book, I'd like to give you some additional useful tips. I suspect you'll find them handy at some point in your work with dBASE II.

Proper Sorting by Date

With dBASE, and computers in general, we usually store dates in a MM/DD/YY format (i.e., 03/31/83). This is a convenient method, but has unpleasant effects on chronological sorts. For example, if we were to create a data base called DATES

CREATE B:DATES <RET>

and fill in the structure as follows:

```
ENTER RECORD STRUCTURE AS FOLLOWS:
FIELD    NAME,TYPE,WIDTH,DECIMAL PLACES
001      DATE,C,8
002      <RET>
```

When dBASE asks

INPUT DATA NOW? (Y/N)

if we answer Y, we could fill in the following dates:

```
01/01/83
01/01/79
02/02/81
02/15/80
02/28/81
03/01/83
03/15/80
03/31/79
04/30/83
04/16/81
04/11/80
04/18/76
```

After entering the dates, we could

USE B:DATES <RET>
LIST <RET>

and we'd see the dates in exactly the same order we typed them.

00001	01/01/83
00002	01/01/79
00003	02/02/81
00004	02/15/80
00005	02/28/81
00006	03/01/83
00007	03/15/80
00008	03/31/79
00009	04/30/83
00010	04/16/81
00011	04/11/80
00012	04/18/76

Now we might want to sort or index by date with the command

INDEX ON DATE TO B:DATES   < RET >

we'd see

00012 RECORDS INDEXED

But if we do a LIST, we'll see the dates sorted by month, not by year.

00002	01/01/79
00001	01/01/83
00003	02/02/81
00004	02/15/80
00005	02/28/81
00006	03/01/83
00007	03/15/80
00008	03/31/79
00011	04/11/80
00010	04/16/81
00012	04/18/76
00009	04/30/83

The sort is correct in the strict sense of the term. That is, the Januarys (01) are above the Februarys (02). However, this is not in proper chronological order. 02/15/80 should come before 01/01/83. The remedy is not as difficult as you might think. All we have to do is make the year more important than the month when sorting. That is, we must put the year before the month. More specifically, we must put the last two characters in the date (YY) in front of the first characters in the date (MM/DD). So when dBASE sorts, the sort uses the format YY/MM/DD. We can use the $ to help with this. This time, if we ask dBASE to

    INDEX ON $(DATE,7,2) + $(DATE,1,6) TO B:DATES

we get the message

00012 RECORDS INDEXED

Now if we do a

    LIST   <RET>

we see that the records are in proper chronological order.

00012   04/18/76
00002   01/01/79
00008   03/31/79
00004   02/15/80
00007   03/15/80
00011   04/11/80
00003   02/02/81
00005   02/28/81
00010   04/16/81
00001   01/01/83
00006   03/01/83
00009   04/30/83

Why? We told dBASE to INDEX ON $(DATE,7,2) + $(DATE,1,6), which translates to indexing on the last two characters in the date, starting at the seventh character, $(DATE,7,2), plus the first six characters + $(DATE,1,6). If we could view the dates in this format, we'd see the year before the month and day.

76/04/18

79/01/01

79/03/31

80/02/15

80/03/15

80/04/11

81/02/02

81/02/28

81/04/16

83/01/01

83/03/01

83/04/30

They sort properly in this format because the year is of primary importance, rather than the month. This only works if you've strictly followed the MM/DD/YY format. For example, if some dates were missing leading zeros, as below:

01/01/83

01/01/79

02/02/81

2/15/80

02/28/81

03/01/83

3/15/80

3/31/79

04/30/83

04/16/81

4/11/80

04/18/76

the sort might not come out properly. We would have to first get these all into MM/DD/YY with the command

> **REPLACE ALL DATE WITH '0' + DATE FOR LEN;**
> **(TRIM(DATE))< 8   <RET>**

That means, "Replace all the dates with a zero padded onto the front of the date in those cases where the length of the date (with the blanks trimmed off) is less than eight characters." LEN is a dBASE function which tells the length of a field, MM/DD/YY format is eight characters long. Doing a LIST now we'd see

```
00001   01/01/83
00002   01/01/79
00003   02/02/81
00004   02/15/80
00005   02/28/81
00006   03/01/83
00007   03/15/80
00008   03/31/79
00009   04/30/83
00010   04/16/81
00011   04/11/80
00012   04/18/76
```

All dates would have leading zeros, and would now sort properly, using the YY/MM/DD format. Any kind of deviation from the MM/DD/YY format might cause additional problems. Your best bet, if you plan on doing any sorting with dates, is to stick to the MM/DD/YY format. Then use the INDEX command above to do the sorting.

Record Numbers in Reports

None of the formatted reports we've shown so far have included record numbers, and there is no indication from the dBASE user's manual that this is feasible. However, it is feasible, and quite easy. All we have to do is put the record number symbol (#) in the column we wish it to appear, and it will show up on the report. For example, if we

USE B:MAIL < RET >

and

REPORT FORM B:RECNO < RET >

and define the format as follows:

```
ENTER OPTIONS, M = LEFT MARGIN, L = LINES/PAGE,
   W = PAGE WIDTH
PAGE HEADING? (Y/N) Y
ENTER PAGE HEADING: Mailing List With Record Numbers
DOUBLE SPACE REPORT? (Y/N) N
ARE TOTALS REQUIRED? (Y/N) N
COL   WIDTH,CONTENTS
001   4,#
ENTER HEADING: Rec No.
002   15,LNAME
ENTER HEADING: Last Name
003   10,FNAME
ENTER HEADING: First Name
004   20,ADDRESS
ENTER HEADING: Address
005   15,PHONE
ENTER HEADING: Phone Number
006
```

we see a report like this:

```
PAGE NO. 00001

                 Mailing List With Record Numbers

Rec
No.   Last Name   First Name   Address          Phone Number
 1    Appleby     Andy         123 A. St.
 2    Smith       John Q.      123 A. St.
```

3	Smithsonian	Lucy	461 Adams St.	
4	Doe	Ruth	1142 J. St.	
5	SMITH	Betsy	222 Lemon Dr.	
6	Rhodes	Dusty	P.O. Box 12345	(213) 555-1212
7	Frisbee	Hobart	321 Third Ave.	(213) 555-0101
8	Johnson	May	123 Oak St.	(111) 111-1111

The record number for each individual appears in the first column of the report, because we put 4,# as the width and contents of COL 001.

Managing Multiple Index Files

There are a couple of tricks to indexing. If we INDEX ON LNAME TO B:NAMES, this will create an index file that tells dBASE the proper order in which to list records alphabetically by last name. However, if we later USE B:MAIL, and append some records, the NAMES index file will not be automatically updated to include the newly appended records. Therefore, if we USE B:MAIL INDEX B:NAMES after adding new records, we're likely to get either unpredictable results, or an error message that reads RECORD OUT OF RANGE. If that should occur, you must re-create the index file by again typing in the command INDEX ON LNAME TO B:NAMES. As a way around this, just prior to appending the new records, ask dBASE to USE B:MAIL INDEX B:NAMES, and *then* append the new records. This way, with both B:MAIL and B:NAMES.NDX in USE when we append, both the B:MAIL data base and the B:NAMES.NDX index are updated whenever we append new records.

Now what about the case where we have a NAMES.NDX index file which has information for printing out records in last name order, and a ZIP.NDX index that has information about displaying records in zip code order? We can make both index files active at the same time by typing in

        USE B:MAIL INDEX B:NAMES, B:ZIP   <RET>

If we type in the above command and do a LIST, the data will be displayed in last name order, since the NAMES index is the master (first-listed) index file. However, if we then APPEND new records, or EDIT records with two index files active like this, both index files will automatically be updated to reflect the new records. If we change fields with BROWSE, READ, or REPLACE with multiple index files active like this, all index files will also be updated accordingly.

Managing multiple index files in this fashion can be a tricky business. Until you're comfortable with indexing, you might be better off reindexing your data bases after appending or changing data on your data base. That is, to add new records to the MAIL data base, just

USE B:MAIL   < RET >

then

APPEND   < RET >

new data into mail. After you are done adding new records, just

INDEX ON LNAME TO B:NAMES   < RET >

and when that index is complete,

INDEX ON ZIP TO B:ZIPS   < RET >

This will decrease the likelihood of encountering errors like RECORD OUT OF RANGE or END OF FILE ENCOUNTERED UNEXPECTEDLY, or multiple records appearing in your displays.

Also, the PACK command does not handle multiple index files in dBase versions previous to 2.4. If you have to PACK an indexed file, reindex all index files after the pack. You might want to create a command file to handle this for you.

Using Abbreviations

To speed up our typing, dBASE allows us to abbreviate commands to four letters. Therefore, we can type in SELE PRIM rather than SELECT PRIMARY to get the same result. Any command can be abbreviated. Here are some common commands and their abbreviations.

COMMAND	ABBREVIATION
SELECT PRIMARY	SELE PRIM
SELECT SECONDARY	SELE SECO
REPORT FORM B:BYNAMES	REPO FORM B:BYNAMES
DELETE RECORD 6	DELE RECO 6
REPLACE ALL LNAME WITH 'Smith'	REPL ALL LNAME WITH 'Smith'
APPEND	APPE
SET DEFAULT TO B	SET DEFA TO B
SET LINKAGE ON	SET LINK ON
MODIFY COMMAND B:LABELS	MODI COMM B:LABELS
MODIFY STRUCTURE	MODI STRU
DISPLAY STRUCTURE	DISP STRU
DISPLAY MEMORY	DISP MEMO

Multi-Column Mailing Labels

Many organizations prefer to use print mailing labels on sheets
that have more than one label across. This is especially needed if the
labels will be photocopied. dBASE has no built-in capability to print
labels in this fashion, but a command file could certainly do it. I've
included a general purpose mailing label program here that can
handle just about any label configuration you might come up with.
It's a bit lengthy so it might take some time to key in. Once it's in, you

can USE (whatever file you're printing labels from) and DO the command file. The file will ask some questions:

```
How many labels across? :0:
How wide each label (X.X inch) :0.0:
Send labels to printer? (Y/N) : :
```

The questions that require numeric answers have zeros holding the place of the answer. Fill in the appropriate answer with a new number to replace the zero. Answer the first question with the number of labels to be printed across each page. For the second question, put in the width of each label. For instance, if the labels are 2½ inches wide, fill in 2.5 (actually, 25; the command file puts in the decimal). If you answer Y to the third question, the screen will ask

```
Pause for paper change between pages? (Y/N)
```

If you are using individual sheets of mailing labels, rather than a continuous form, answer Y to this question, and the screen will ask

```
How many labels per page? : 1:
```

Most individual sheets have eleven rows of labels on them, but it's pretty hard to line up the sheets to get all eleven rows printed. You might want to try typing 10 here.

If the labels are being sent to the printer, this message will appear next:

```
Line up labels in printer and press RETURN
```

Put in the labels and press RETURN. If you are using individual sheets, the command file will print a sheet of labels, eject it, then ask you to

```
Enter new page and press any key to continue.
WAITING
```

At which point you should put the next sheet in the printer, and press any key to print the next page of labels.

This program assumes that your printer is set to ten characters to the inch. Here are some labels printed three across. Each label is 2.5 inches wide, as printed by the command file.

Andy Appleby	John Q. Smith	Lucy Smithsonian
123 A. St.	123 A. St.	461 Adams St.
San Diego, CA 92123	San Diego, CA 92122	San Diego, CA 92122
Ruth Doe	Betsy SMITH	Dusty Rhodes
1142 J. St.	222 Lemon Dr.	P.O. Box 12345
Los Angeles, CA 91234	New York, NY 01234	Los Angeles, CA 91234
Hobart Frisbee	May Johnson	
321 Third Ave.	123 Oak St.	
Cucamonga, CA 91234	Boston, MA 01234	

When all the labels have been printed, this message is displayed:

Done with labels

The command file to print labels in this fashion is shown in Program 17.1. Although it is lengthy and slow, it can handle all types of mailing labels, so if you need this flexibility, it's probably worth taking the time to key it in.

```
            ******************* Multi-Column Mailing Labels.
      SET TALK OFF
      ERASE
      STORE 0.0 TO ACROSS,WIDE,LCOUNT
      STORE 1 TO PER:PAGE
      STORE ' ' TO LP,PCHANGE

      ********** Get label format information.
      a 1,1 SAY 'How many labels across? ' GET ACROSS PICTURE '9'
      a 2,1 SAY 'How wide each label? (X.X inch) ' GET WIDE PICTURE '9.9'
      a 4,1 SAY 'Send labels to printer? (Y/N) ' GET LP
      READ

      ********** Ask about pagination.
      IF !(LP)='Y'
          a 6,1 SAY 'Pause for paper change between pages? (Y/N) ' GET PCHANGE
          READ

          IF !(PCHANGE)='Y'
              a 7,1 SAY 'How many labels per page? ' GET PER:PAGE PICTURE '99'
              READ
```

─Program 17.1─

```
      ENDIF (pchange=y)
   ENDIF (lp=y)

   **************************** Handle printer, if necessary.
   ERASE
   IF !(LP)='Y'
      ACCEPT ' Line up labels in printer and press RETURN ' TO NOTHING
      ERASE
      SET PRINT ON
   ENDIF (lp=y)


   *********************************************************************
   *                    Label Printing Routine                        *
   *********************************************************************
   GO TOP
   DO WHILE .NOT. EOF

      ********************** Store individual label data to memory variables.
      STORE 1 TO COUNTER
      DO WHILE COUNTER <= ACROSS .AND. .NOT. EOF
         STORE STR(COUNTER,1) TO S1
         STORE '1' TO S2
         STORE TRIM(FNAME)+' ' + LNAME TO LAB&S1&S2
         STORE '2' TO S2
         STORE ADDRESS TO LAB&S1&S2
         STORE '3' TO S2
         STORE TRIM(CITY)+', '+TRIM(STATE)+'  '+ZIP TO LAB&S1&S2
         STORE COUNTER + 1 TO COUNTER
         SKIP
      ENDDO (while counter <= across and not eof)

      ********************** Pad/truncate label data to proper length.
      STORE 1 TO OL
      DO WHILE OL <= ACROSS
         STORE STR(OL,1) TO S1
         STORE 1 TO IL
         DO WHILE IL < 4
            STORE STR(IL,1) TO S2
            DO WHILE LEN(LAB&S1&S2) < WIDE*10
               STORE LAB&S1&S2 + ' ' TO LAB&S1&S2
            ENDDO (while too short)
            STORE $(LAB&S1&S2,1,WIDE*10) TO LAB&S1&S2
            STORE IL+1 TO IL
         ENDDO (while il < 4)
         STORE OL+1 TO OL
      ENDDO (while ol < across)

      ****************** Now do the actual printing.
      STORE 1 TO OL
      DO WHILE OL < 4
         STORE 1 TO IL
         STORE STR(OL,1) TO S2
         STORE STR(IL,1) TO S1
```

Program 17.1 (continued)

```
    ? LAB&S1&S2
    STORE 2 TO IL
    DO WHILE IL <=ACROSS
        STORE STR(IL,1) TO S1
        ?? LAB&S1&S2
        STORE IL+1 TO IL
    ENDDO (il)
    STORE OL+1 TO OL
ENDDO (ol)
?
?
?
STORE LCOUNT+1 TO LCOUNT

**************** Check for paper change.
IF !(PCHANGE)='Y' .AND. (LCOUNT/PER:PAGE)=INT(LCOUNT/PER:PAGE)
    EJECT
    SET PRINT OFF
    ERASE
    ? 'Enter new page and press any key to continue.'
    WAIT TO NOTHING
    SET PRINT ON
ENDIF (pchange = y and labels evenly divisible by per:page)

****************** Clear labels to avoid repeats.
STORE 1 TO OL
DO WHILE OL <= ACROSS
    STORE STR(OL,1) TO S1
    STORE 1 TO IL
    DO WHILE IL < 4
        STORE STR(IL,1) TO S2
        STORE ' ' TO LAB&S1&S2
        STORE IL+1 TO IL
    ENDDO (il)
        STORE OL+1 TO OL
        ENDDO (ol)
    ENDDO (while not eof)

    ********************* Done with labels.
    SET PRINT OFF
    ?
    ?
    ? ' Done with labels'
```

Program 17.1 (continued)

Where Do I Go from Here?

Practice.   The only way to become fluent in a new language (such as dBASE II) is to use it. Create a data base and work with it. If you're worried about experimenting on important data, just make a backup of the data base first (COPY TO B:TEMP). Then, if you make a mess on the original data file, just DELETE ALL of the records from it, PACK it, and APPEND FROM TEMP. It's always a good idea to COPY TO B:TEMP when you work with a data base. If anything at all goes wrong, including a power shortage, you have the security of a backup.

Read the manual.   Few of us can stand to drudge through a technical user's manual, but it is important to do so to get a feel for all the capabilities and rules of this software. In this book, we've covered most of the dBASE II commands, and have tried to demonstrate their use through practical exercises. Read the manual to get additional information and more examples of commands.

Pace yourself.   Don't try to work out problems that are over your head at the outset, or else you'll just end up frustrated. Learning to master the marvelous machine can be very enjoyable if you pace yourself. Work at a comfortable level and experiment to learn more. If you make it fun, you'll learn more in the long run.

INTERFACING dBASE II WITH OTHER SOFTWARE SYSTEMS

A

We can combine dBASE power with other software systems by transferring files to and from dBASE. In this appendix, we will discuss transferring data between dBASE and word processors, using the WordStar program as the example. We will also discuss transfer methods for spreadsheets, using the SuperCalc package as an example. We will then discuss transferring BASIC data files.

Interfacing with Word Processors

We can send dBASE reports to word processing systems for further editing or inclusion in other documents. To do so, we design our report using the REPORT command in dBASE. Then prior to printing the report, with dBASE's dot prompt showing, we SET ALTERNATE TO (some data file name). We then SET ALTERNATE ON, and generate the report. Then we SET ALTERNATE OFF, and QUIT dBASE. We can then load up our word processor, and read the report into the word processing system. Here is a typical scenario using the WordStar program as the word processor.

```
A>  DBASE    <RET>
.
USE  B:MAIL
REPORT  FORM  B:BYNAME    <RET>

(fill  in  report  characteristics
  if  necessary)

SET  ALTERNATE  TO  B:TRANSFER    <RET>
SET  ALTERNATE  ON    <RET>
REPORT  FORM  B:BYNAME    <RET>
SET  ALTERNATE  OFF    <RET>
QUIT    <RET>

A>
```

When we set alternate to TRANSFER, dBASE created a disk file called TRANSFER.TXT. When we SET ALTERNATE ON, dBASE sent all information that appeared on the screen to the file TRANSFER.TXT. When we SET ALTERNATE OFF, no more information was set to TRANSFER.TXT. When we QUIT dBASE, the A> reappeared on the screen. Now we can load up WordStar. Let's say we want to pull the dBASE report into a document called MANUAL.TXT. We'd type in

```
WS B:MANUAL.TXT   <RET>
```

When the document appears on the screen, position the cursor to the place that you want the dBASE report to appear. Then enter a

```
^KR
```

The WordStar program asks NAME OF FILE TO READ? We reply with

TRANSFER.TXT   < RET >

That's all there is to it. The report which appeared on the screen when we asked dBASE to REPORT FORM B:BYNAME is now in our WordStar document, and is also in a disk file called TRANSFER.TXT.

Now, we may want to send our dBASE file to WordStar's MailMerge option for printing form letters. In this case, we need to create a data base in MailMerge format. Let's say that we want to send our MAIL data base to a MailMerge file from which to print form letters. After loading up dBASE, type in

USE B:MAIL   < RET >

Then we need to COPY it to another data file in MailMerge readable form. The command is

COPY TO B:MM DELIMITED WITH ,   < RET >

This creates a data file called MM.TXT which the MailMerge file can access to create form letters. Then we would have to create the form letter in WordStar. Recall that our MAIL data base contains the fields LNAME, FNAME, ADDRESS, CITY, STATE, ZIP, PHONE. We would have to QUIT dBASE and load up the WordStar program. Then we could create a document called B:FORM.LET. Program A.1 contains a FORM.LET which can read the data file we've just created:

```
.OP
.DF B:MM.TXT
.RV LNAME,FNAME,ADDRESS,CITY,STATE,ZIP,PHONE

&FNAME& &LNAME&
&ADDRESS&
&CITY&, &STATE&       &ZIP&

Dear &FNAME&,

        How do you like getting these form letters? You
probably wouldn't know the difference if it were not
for my dot matrix printer.

                Ta ta for now,

                Zeppo
```

————Program A.1————

Notice that we've included PHONE in the .RV command, even though it is not used in the form letter anywhere. This is essential if the PHONE variable exists. The .RV command is expecting a certain number of fields, so it must have the same number of fields as the data file, regardless of whether or not we plan on using that field in our form letter. Even if we only wanted the first name for our form letter, we would still need to read in all of the fields. If you forget this important tidbit, your form letter might come out in a most unpleasant format.

After we create and save the form letter, we merely need to merge print it using the appropriate MailMerge command. That is, select WordStar option M from the WordStar Main Menu, and when it asks NAME OF FILE TO MERGE PRINT?, tell it B:FORM.LET < RET >. A letter for each individual in the MAIL data base will then be printed. Here is how the first one should come out:

Andy Appleby

123 A. St.

San Diego, CA 92123

Dear Andy,

How do you like getting these form letters? You probably wouldn't know the difference if it were not for my dot matrix printer.

Ta ta for now,

Zeppo

We could use our LABELS program to print mailing labels for all these individuals, or we could create a WordStar MailMerge document to print names and addresses directly on envelopes, one envelope at a time. In Program A.2 is a MailMerge file to print envelopes from our MM.TXT data file, which we'll call ENVEL.TXT.

After we create and save ENVEL.TXT, we can merge print it in the usual WordStar fashion. However, when the merge print option asks "PAUSE FOR PAPER CHANGE BETWEEN PAGES? (Y/N)," be sure to answer Y. Then, you can insert each individual envelope, lining it up so that the printer head is right where you want the printing to start. The MailMerge option will print one envelope, eject it from the printer, and wait for you to put in the next envelope.

If you want your form letter to go to certain individuals only, you can specify this in your dBASE COPY command. Let's assume we want our form letters to go to San Diego residents only. With the dBASE dot prompt showing, and the MAIL data base in use, type in the command

    COPY TO B:MM FOR CITY = 'San Diego' DELIMITED WITH ,
        <RET>

Only San Diego residents would appear on the MailMerge file, hence only individuals in San Diego would have form letters printed.

There is one slight catch, however. If a single field has a comma embedded in it, it will cause some problems with the form letters. A partial solution would be to use the command

    COPY TO B:MM DELIMITED WITH "   <RET>

This command has the negative effect of padding all the data in the MM.TXT file with trailing blanks. The only compromise here is to purchase a program that takes care of these problems for you. Fox and Gellar's Quickcode program will handle most MailMerge problems that you might have.

If you already have a MailMerge file and want to use some dBASE commands to manage it, you can send a copy of it to dBASE. To do so, you need to load up dBASE and CREATE an empty file with the CREATE command. Structure it so that it has the same fields as your

```
.MT 0
.OP
.DF B:MM.TXT
.RV LNAME,FNAME,ADDRESS,CITY,STATE,ZIP,PHONE

              &FNAME& &LNAME&
              &ADDRESS&
              &CITY&, &STATE&    &ZIP&

.PA
```

Program A.2

MailMerge file. When dBASE asks INPUT DATA NOW?, say N. Then USE the newly created data base, and

APPEND FROM B:MM.DAT DELIMITED   < RET>

You can now sort your MailMerge file or do whatever you please with it in dBASE II. (This example assumed that the name of your existing MailMerge file was MM.DAT.) To get the dBASE data base back into MailMerge readable form, just USE the dBASE file and

COPY TO B:MM.DAT DELIMITED WITH ,   < RET>

Interfacing with Spreadsheet Software

For our spreadsheet example, we will use the SuperCalc package as the model. First, we will deal with getting information out of SuperCalc into dBASE. To do so, we need to load up the SuperCalc program and read in the desired file with the usual /L command. Next we need to get rid of borders because dBASE can't handle these. Use the SuperCalc /GLOBAL BORDER command to get rid of the borders. Then we need to create an ASCII file of the data in SuperCalc. To do so, use the /O command as usual. Use the D for (D)isplay, and inform SuperCalc of the range (e.g., A1:E25). Then a prompt will ask if you want the data output to screen, printer or disk. Choose D for disk. When SuperCalc asks for the file name, give it any name you wish. We'll use DBCALC for our example. The SuperCalc package will add the extension .PRN to our file name. If you want to store the DBCALC file on drive B, use B:DBCALC as the filename.

Now DBCALC.PRN exists as an ASCII file, and can be read directly into a WordStar document if desired. To get this file into dBASE requires a little more juggling.

First, we need to load up dBASE so that the dot prompt is showing. Then, we need to CREATE a data base that will pull in our SuperCalc file. The data base we create must have a field for each column in the SuperCalc file. In our example we have five columns. I know this because the range I asked to have SuperCalc output was from A1 to E25, and E is the fifth letter of the alphabet.

We need to be careful about data types and widths here. The dBASE field widths must be identical to the SuperCalc column widths. We can see the width of each column in a SuperCalc file by simply placing the SuperCalc cursor under each field. Let's say our SuperCalc file had the first field as account number, the second as account title, the third as MTD balance, the fourth as QTD balance, and the fifth field as YTD balance. We would need to structure our dBASE file as follows:

```
FIELD       NAME,TYPE,WIDTH,DECIMAL PLACES
001         ACCNO,N,6,2
002         TITLE,C,20,0
003         MTD,N,12,2
004         QTD,N,12,2
005         YTD,N,12,2
006
INPUT DATA NOW? N
```

Now we need to USE this newly created file and

APPEND FROM DBCALC.PRN SDF   < RET>

Now we can dBASE a copy of our SuperCalc file to our heart's content.

Interfacing with BASIC Data Files

The BASIC language allows you to create data files with either variable-length records (sequential files), or fixed-length records (random access data files). Sequential files are easy to deal with. To send dBASE files to BASIC sequential data files, we merely need to load up dBASE, USE the data file of interest, then

COPY TO BASIC.DAT SDF DELIMITED WITH "   < RET>

This will work fine for MBASIC or CBASIC sequential files. To read BASIC sequential data files into dBASE, we must load up dBASE, and CREATE a data base with a structure that matches the BASIC file.

Then, we just

APPEND FROM BASIC.DAT DELIMITED   <RET>

dBASE will then treat the new version of the BASIC data file as one of its own.

Random access files may present more of a problem. MBASIC stores its random access files in binary notation, undelimited with fixed field lengths and no carriage return line/feed at the end. This is indeed a problem. The easiest method for getting an MBASIC random access file into a dBASE data base might be to first create a sequential file from the random access file in BASIC, then just read the data into dBASE using the commands mentioned above. An MBASIC program capable of performing such a feat is shown in Program A.3.

```
   10 REM ********** Send Random Access data to a sequential file
   20 OPEN "R", #1, "RFILE.DAT", 60
   25 FIELD #1, 20 AS F1$, 10 AS F2$, 15 AS F3$, 9 AS F4$,
      5 AS F5$, 10 AS F6$, 30 AS F7$

   30 OPEN "O", #2, "SFILE.DAT"

   40 FOR REC% = 1 TO 90000
   50     GOSUB 1000    :REM Read next R/A record
   55     REM **************** Assumes a zero marks the last record
   60     IF LNAME$="0" THEN 100
   70     WRITE #2, LNAME$,FNAME$,ADDRESS$,CITY$,STATE$,ZIP$,PHONE$
   80 NEXT REC%

   90 REM ******** Done with transfer

  100 CLOSE
  110 SYSTEM

 1000 REM ****** Read random access record
 1010 GET #1,REC%
 1020 LNAME$=F1$
 1030 FNAME$=F2$
 1040 ADDRESS$=F3$
 1050 CITY$=F4$
 1060 STATE$=F5$
 1070 ZIP$=F6$
 1080 PHONE$=F7$
 1090 RETURN
```

Program A.3

To send dBASE data into an MBASIC random access file, we could use the COPY command mentioned above, then treat it as a sequential file, and write an MBASIC program to translate the MBASIC sequential file to an MBASIC random file. In Program A.4, you will see the MBASIC code for that.

CBASIC and CB-80 handle random access files a little differently. Random files are stored in ASCII, delimited with commas, with variable-length fields. CBASIC random files will read a dBASE program that has been copied to another file delimited OK, but then the CBASIC or CB-80 program needs to deal with the nuisance of the padded fields. An easier way around this is to have dBASE mimic the CBASIC or CB-80 compiler. We need to CREATE a dBASE data base with one field, with the total length of the fields equalling the record length of the CBASIC random access file. In the code below, we will

```
    10 REM ********** Send Sequential data to a Random file
    20 OPEN "R", #1, "RFILE.DAT", 60
    25 FIELD #1, 20 AS F1$, 10 AS F2$, 15 AS F3$, 9 AS F4$,
       5 AS F5$, 10 AS F6$, 30 AS F7$

    30 OPEN "O", #2, "SFILE.DAT"

    40 FOR REC% = 1 TO 90000
    50    IF EOF(2) THEN 100
    60    INPUT #2, LNAME$,FNAME$,ADDRESS$,CITY$,STATE$,ZIP$,PHONE$
    70    GOSUB 1000     :REM Write next R/A record
    80 NEXT REC%

    90 REM ******** Done with transfer

    100 CLOSE
    110 SYSTEM

    1000 REM ****** Read Random access record
    1010 LSET LNAME$=F1$
    1020 LSET FNAME$=F2$
    1030 LSET ADDRESS$=F3$
    1040 LSET CITY$=F4$
    1050 LSET STATE$=F5$
    1060 LSET ZIP$=F6$
    1070 LSET PHONE$=F7$
    1080 PUT #1,REC%
    1090 RETURN
```

Program A.4

assume that the dBASE file CBASIC.DAT has already been created
accordingly. (We're assuming here that if you have enough computer
sophistication to write a random access data file system in CBASIC or
CB-80, you don't need step-by-step instructions to create the appropriate data base). Now, using our MAIL.DBF data base as an example, we
can write the routine in Program A.5 to create true CBASIC/CB-80 random access data files.

```
    SELECT PRIMARY
USE B:MAIL

    SELECT SECONDARY
USE B:CBASIC.DAT

    SELECT PRIMARY

DO WHILE .NOT. EOF
    SELECT SECONDARY
    APPEND BLANK
    STORE TRIM(LNAME) + ','+TRIM(FNAME)+','+TRIM(ADDRESS)+',';
          +TRIM(CITY)+','+TRIM(STATE)+','+TRIM(ZIP)+',';
          +TRIM(PHONE) TO CRECORD

    ******************** Pad entire record with blanks
    DO WHILE LEN(CRECORD) < 155
       STORE CRECORD + ' ' TO CRECORD
    ENDDO

    REPLACE CBFIELD WITH CRECORD

    SELECT PRIMARY
ENDDO  (while not EOF)
USE
QUIT
```

—*Program A.5*—

Now the entire CBASIC.DAT file can be copied to another file with
the SDF option and put in ASCII to get rid of the dBASE header. You
may have to experiment with this a bit, but if you're already working
with CB-80 random access files, I suspect that the experimentation will
not take too long.

Pascal, PL/1, and other language programmers can follow the steps
provided for MBASIC and CBASIC data files to work out a method for
interfacing dBASE data bases with their compilers.

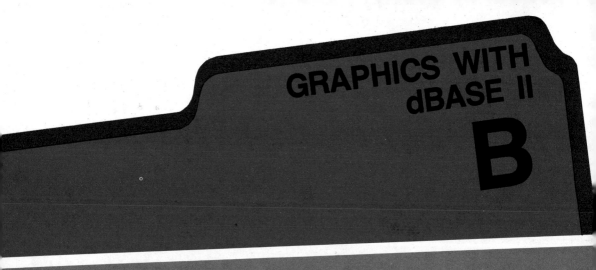

GRAPHICS WITH dBASE II

B

You might ask, "Since when does one do graphics with a data base management system?" We're not talking about doing anything too fancy here, just drawing some pictures or perhaps a bar graph on the screen. We can't use any high-resolution graphics here either, just the computer's standard character set.

The Character Set

The first thing we need to know about our machine is what characters we have to work with. Obviously we can use the ones on our keyboard, but most computers and printers have extra graphics characters hidden away in their memories. We can pull the little devils out of hiding with the CHR function. The CHR function tells us the character that goes along with a number. For instance, CHR(42) is an asterisk, CHR(32) is a blank space. Each letter and number on the keyboard is assigned an ASCII number, and the CHR function translates a number into its appropriate character. ASCII stands for American Standard Code for Information Interchange, a standard for assigning numbers to characters on computer keyboards. We can see the ASCII character set just by writing and doing the command file in Program B.1.

```
******** Generate ASCII Chart.
SET TALK OFF
? ' ASCII Character Set'
?

STORE 32 TO COUNTER
DO WHILE COUNTER < 128
    ? STR(COUNTER,3) + '. ' + CHR(COUNTER)
    STORE COUNTER + 1 TO COUNTER
ENDDO
```

Program B.1

When we DO this command file, we get the following results:

ASCII Character Set

32.

33. !

34. "

35. #

36. $

37. %

38. &

39. '

40. (

41.)

42. *

43. +

44. ,

45. –

46. .

etc.

Where are all the fancy graphics characters? They are hidden away in numbers greater than 127, beyond the standard character set. I can't guarantee that your particular terminal has a graphics set, so don't be disappointed if you don't get good results. The characters whiz by on the screen pretty fast, so let's create the command file in Program B.2 with three columns so that more characters are displayed on the screen.

This will yield an unpredictable result, but mine came out looking like those in Figure B.1.

You will probably notice that if you SET PRINT ON before printing the ASCII chart, the graphics characters look different on the screen than on the printed copy. This is because the ASCII numbers above 127 are free turf for manufacturers, so different companies assign different characters to these ASCII numbers. Keep a copy of your graphics chart on paper. When you want to use a graphics character, you can just look up its number, and tell dBASE to ? CHR(___).

```
    ********************Display Graphics set
    ERASE
    SET TALK OFF
    ? 'Graphics characters'
    ?
    STORE 127 TO N

    DO WHILE N < 255
        ? STR(N,3)+CHR(N)+'   '+STR(N+1,3)+CHR(N+1)+'   '+STR(N+2,3)+CHR(N+2)
        STORE N+3 TO N
    ENDDO
```

Program B.2

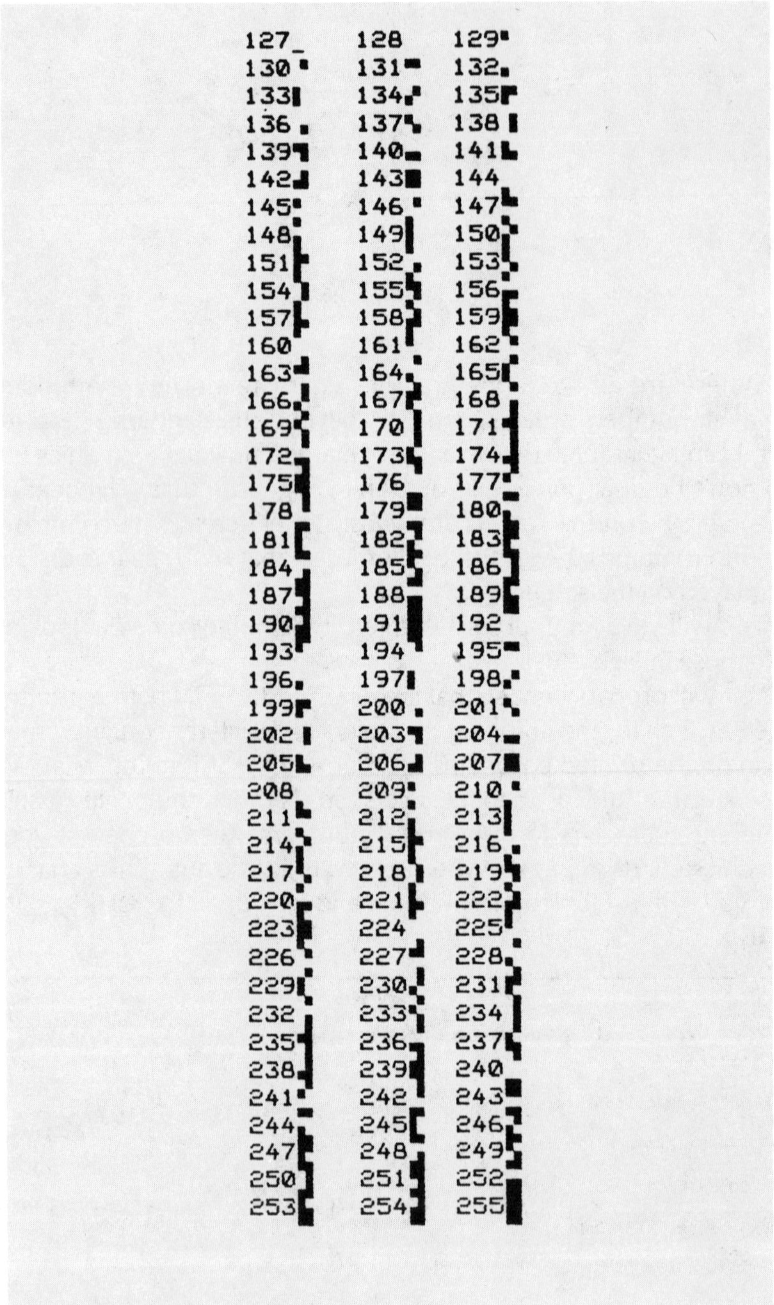

Figure B.1: Graphics Characters

Drawing Pictures on the Screen

Suppose I want to draw Figure B.2 on the screen. Frivolous, you say? Yes indeed.

Ideally, we would draw the picture on a piece of graph paper, and put each asterisk in a separate box on the paper. Now, we can easily see the row and column number of each character. Doing things the hard way, we could then write a command file that says

```
@  1,1  SAY  '*'
@  1,2  SAY  '*'
@  1,3  SAY  '*'
```

etc., but that is too many @ R,C SAY '*' to write. Instead, we will CREATE a data base called FACE and structure it as such:

FIELD   NAME,TYPE,WIDTH,DECIMAL PLACES

00001   ROW,N,3,0

00002   COL,N,3,0

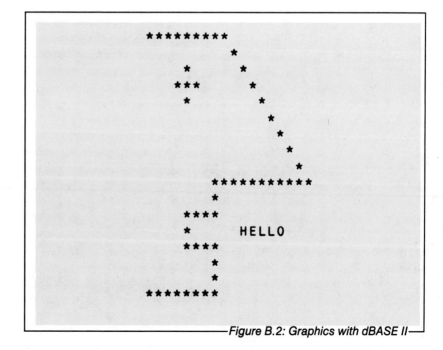

Figure B.2: Graphics with dBASE II

Then we can APPEND our coordinates into the data base, each as a record.

ROW	COL
1	1
1	2
1	3
1	4
1	5
1	6
1	7
1	8
1	9
2	10
3	11
4	12
5	13
6	14
7	15
8	16
8	15
8	14
8	13
8	12
8	11
8	10
8	9
9	9
10	9
11	9
11	8
11	7
11	6
12	6
13	6

14	6
14	7
14	8
14	9
15	9
16	9
17	9
17	8
17	7
17	6
17	5
17	4
17	3
17	2
17	1
3	5
4	4
4	5
4	6
5	5

Now we can create a command file that draws from the data we put in the FACE data base. This is shown in Program B.3.

```
*********** Draw a data base's contents.
ERASE
SET TALK OFF
USE B:FACE
DO WHILE .NOT. EOF
    a ROW,COL SAY '*'
    SKIP 1
ENDDO
a 12,11 SAY 'HELLO'
```

Program B.3

When we DO DRAW, we get the face displayed on the screen. We could also make a general-purpose command file, as shown in Program B.4, that could draw the contents of any data base. This would allow us to make up even more amusing pictures.

To send pictures to the printer, just SET FORMAT TO PRINT above the 'DO WHILE' loop. After the picture is drawn, SET FORMAT TO SCREEN, as in the routine in Program B.5.

A General-Purpose Bar Graph Routine

Before you spend a bundle on a graphics package for your computer, you might want to try keying in GRAPH.CMD, the command

```
******** Draw requested picture
ERASE
SET TALK OFF
ACCEPT 'Use which data base' TO FILENAME
USE &FILENAME
ERASE
DO WHILE .NOT. EOF
    a ROW,COL SAY '*'
    SKIP 1
ENDDO
```

Program B.4

```
******** Draw requested picture
ERASE
SET FORMAT TO PRINT

DO WHILE .NOT. EOF
    a ROW,COL SAY '*'
    SKIP 1
ENDDO
SET FORMAT TO SCREEN

RETURN
```

Program B.5

file I've listed on the last few pages of this appendix. Once you get it typed in and saved (under the file name GRAPH.CMD), you can DO it with dBASE, and it will ask the following series of questions:

```
Enter graph title :
How many columns? :
How wide each column? :
Enter low end of Y axis :
Enter high end of Y axis :
```

Just answer each question as it appears on the screen, and follow your answer with RETURN. Let's say you want to title your graph "Sample Graph" and plot six columns of data on it, each column ten spaces wide. On the Y (vertical) axis, you want the low end to be zero and the high end to be 100. Just answer each question as follows:

```
Enter graph title : Sample    <RET>
How many columns? : 6    <RET>
How wide each column? : 10    <RET>
Enter low end of Y axis : 0    <RET>
Enter high end of Y axis : 100    <RET>
```

At that point the screen will clear and GRAPH will ask for the value to be plotted in each column, like so:

```
Column 1 data? :
Column 2 data? :
Column 3 data? :
Column 4 data? :
Column 5 data? :
Column 6 data? :
```

Make sure you key in values within the Y-axis range you've specified (0–100 in this example). Then, GRAPH will plot the graph on your screen for you. When it is done, it will just stay there until you press the RETURN key. At that point, the screen will clear, and ask

Send Graph to printer? (Y/N) :

If you answer Y, the graph will then be sent to your printer. Below, I've provided a sample graph in Figure B.3, created on my Okidata Microline printer with GRAPH.CMD.

The GRAPH.CMD command file is also presented, with some notes on configuring it to other printers and terminals. Enjoy!

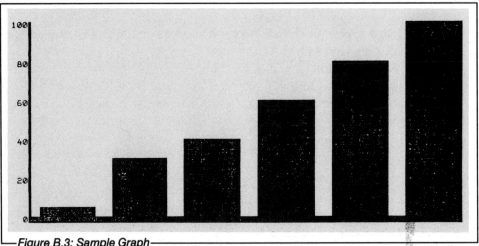

└─*Figure B.3: Sample Graph*─

Sample Graphs

Here's the entire GRAPH command file. Inside the program, notice the graphics characters used for the screen are set up in the routine.

```
    ************************************************
    * GRAPH.CMD                                    *
    * Create a custom bar graph on screen & printer. *
    ************************************************

    ERASE
    SET TALK OFF
    SET BELL OFF
    SET COLON OFF
```

└─*Program B.6*─

```
*********************************** Get Graph data.
ERASE
ACCEPT 'Enter graph title ' TO TITLE
INPUT ' How many columns ' TO NO:COL
INPUT ' How wide each column ' TO COL:WIDTH
INPUT ' Enter low end of Y axis ' TO LR
INPUT ' Enter high end of Y axis ' TO HR
ERASE
STORE 1 TO LP
DO WHILE LP < NO:COL+1
   STORE STR(LP,2) TO LPS
   IF LP < 10
      STORE $(LPS,2,1) TO LPS
   ENDIF
   STORE '      ' TO COL&LPS
   @ LP,1 SAY ' Column ' +LPS+' data? ' GET COL&LPS PICTURE '999999'
   READ
   STORE LP+1 TO LP
ENDDO

ERASE

*************************** Store graphics characters for screen.
STORE STR(45,3) TO XCHAR
STORE STR(129,3) TO YCHAR
STORE STR(150,3) TO BCHAR

*********************** Create vertical lines.
STORE 1 TO CNTR
STORE ' ' + CHR(&YCHAR) TO LINE

*********************** Create horizontal line.
STORE+' '+CHR(&XCHAR) TO TLINE
STORE 1 TO CNTR
DO WHILE CNTR < NO:COL*COL:WIDTH
   STORE TLINE+CHR(&XCHAR) TO TLINE
   STORE CNTR+1 TO CNTR
ENDDO (while cntr < col*width)

*********************** Create bar character.
STORE ' ' TO BAR
STORE 1 TO CNTR
DO WHILE CNTR < COL:WIDTH-1
   STORE BAR + CHR(&BCHAR) TO BAR
   STORE CNTR+1 TO CNTR
ENDDO (while cntr < width)

*********************** Draw graph background on screen.
ERASE
STORE 1 TO CNTR
STORE 0 TO BCOUNT
?
```

Program B.6 (continued)

```
DO WHILE CNTR < 21
   STORE '    ' TO LEFT
   IF ((CNTR-1)/4 = INT((CNTR-1)/4)) .OR. CNTR = 1
      IF CNTR < 20
         STORE STR(HR-((BCOUNT/5)*HR),5) TO LEFT
         STORE BCOUNT+1 TO BCOUNT
      ENDIF (cntr < 21)
   ENDIF (cntr-1 evenly divisible by 4)
   ? LEFT + LINE
   STORE CNTR+1 TO CNTR
ENDDO (while cntr < 21 lines printed)
? STR(LR,5) + TLINE

****************** Set up looping variables for graph.
STORE 7 TO C
STORE 'COL' TO VBASE
STORE ' ' TO VNAME
STORE (HR-LR)/10 TO DIV
STORE 1 TO OUTLOOP

***************** Set up outer loop.
DO WHILE OUTLOOP < NO:COL+1
   STORE 1 TO CW
   IF OUTLOOP > 9
      STORE 2 TO CW
   ENDIF (outloop > width)
   STORE VBASE + STR(OUTLOOP,CW) TO VNAME
   @ 21,C SAY ' '
   STORE 2*(&&VNAME/DIV) TO COL
   STORE 21 TO ROW

   ****************** Draw bars on screen.
   DO WHILE COL > 0
      @ ROW,C SAY BAR
      STORE ROW - 1 TO ROW
      STORE COL - 1 TO COL
   ENDDO (While COL > 0)
STORE C + COL:WIDTH TO C
STORE OUTLOOP + 1 TO OUTLOOP
ENDDO  (outloop)

****************** Center title over graph.
@ 0,(((NO:COL+1)*COL:WIDTH)/2)-(LEN(TITLE)/2) SAY TITLE
@ 22,0 SAY ' '

******************************** Prepare for printer copy.

ACCEPT TO NOTHING
ERASE
ACCEPT 'Send graph to printer? (Y/N) ' TO YN
ERASE

IF !(YN)='Y'
```

Program B.6 (continued)

```
******************** Set up graphics characters for printer.
STORE STR(143,3) TO XCHAR
STORE STR(213,3) TO YCHAR
STORE STR(255,3) TO BCHAR
STORE CHR(&XCHAR) TO TLINE
STORE 1 TO CNTR

******************** Create printer bottom line.
DO WHILE CNTR < (NO:COL*(COL:WIDTH+1))-1
   STORE TLINE+CHR(&XCHAR) TO TLINE
   STORE CNTR+1 TO CNTR
ENDDO (while cntr < col*width)

**************** Create printer bar.
STORE 1 TO CNTR
STORE ' ' TO BAR
STORE ' ' TO SPACES
DO WHILE CNTR < COL:WIDTH-1
   STORE BAR + CHR(&BCHAR) TO BAR
   STORE SPACES + ' ' TO SPACES
   STORE CNTR + 1 TO CNTR
ENDDO (while cntr < width)

***************************************************************
Generate printer graph.                                      *
***************************************************************

***************************** Center title on printer graph.
  STORE ' ' TO TCENTER
  DO WHILE LEN(TCENTER) < (((NO:COL+1)*COL:WIDTH)/2)-(.5*LEN(TITLE))
     STORE TCENTER + ' ' TO TCENTER
  ENDDO  (len tcenter)
  SET PRINT ON
  ? TCENTER + TITLE
  ?
******************** Start graph loops.
STORE 1 TO LCOUNT
STORE 1 TO CCOUNT
STORE 0 TO BCOUNT

DO WHILE LCOUNT < 21
   STORE '    ' TO LEFT
   IF ((LCOUNT-1)/4 = INT((LCOUNT-1)/4)) .OR. LCOUNT =1
     IF LCOUNT < 20
        STORE STR(HR-((BCOUNT/5)*HR),5) TO LEFT
        STORE BCOUNT+1 TO BCOUNT
     ENDIF (lcount < 20)
   ENDIF (lcount-1 evenly divisble by 4)
     STORE LEFT+ CHR(&YCHAR) TO GLINE
     DO WHILE CCOUNT < NO:COL+1
        STORE 1 TO CW
        IF CCOUNT > 9
           STORE 2 TO CW
```

Program B.6 (continued)

```
        ENDIF (ccount > width)
        STORE 'COL' + STR(CCOUNT,CW) TO VNAME
        IF LCOUNT > 20-(2*(&&VNAME/DIV)))
            STORE GLINE + BAR TO GLINE
        ELSE
            STORE GLINE + SPACES TO GLINE
        ENDIF (lcount > 20)

        STORE GLINE + '  ' TO GLINE
        STORE CCOUNT+1 TO CCOUNT
    ENDDO (for ccount)

    ? GLINE
    STORE ' ' TO GLINE
    STORE 1 TO CCOUNT
    STORE LCOUNT + 1 TO LCOUNT
  ENDDO   (for lcount)

******************* Done with printer graph, print bottom lines.
? STR(LR,5)+ TLINE
?
?
SET PRINT OFF
ENDIF  (if printer was selected)
RETURN
```

—*Program B.6 (continued)*—

```
     ****** Set up graphics characters for printer.
STORE STR(143,3) TO XCHAR
STORE STR(213,3) TO YCHAR
STORE STR(255,3) TO BCHAR
```

That is, I use an ASCII 45 for the X character (X-axis line), an ASCII 129 for the Y-character (Y-axis line), and an ASCII 150 for the bar itself. For the printer, I use these characters (stored in a routine near the middle of the command file).

```
     ****** Store graphics characters for screen.
STORE STR(45,3) TO XCHAR
STORE STR(129,3) TO YCHAR
STORE STR(150,3) TO BCHAR
```

If this program doesn't work, or if your graph comes out looking funny, you may want to try different ASCII characters. You should use the command file at the beginning of this appendix to display the screen and printer character sets for you.

dBASE II
VOCABULARY
C

Command	Definition
!	Displays a field's contents in uppercase [LIST !(LNAME)].
#	Not equal to.
#	Refers to record number (? #, LIST FOR # < 10).
$	Substring function, used for finding a character string embedded within a larger character string (LIST FOR 'Lemon' $ADDRESS).
&	Used for macro substitution (IF &FLD = '&COND'). Macros must be stored in memory variables as character strings.
()	Used for logical and mathematical grouping [? (10+10)*5].
*	Multiplies two numbers (? 10*10).
*	Marks records for deletion. Can also be used to display deleted records (LIST FOR *).
+	Adds two numbers, or links two character strings together (? 10+10).
−	Subtracts two numbers or links two character strings with trailing blanks removed.
.AND.	Two things true simultaneously (LIST FOR 'Oak' $ADDRESS .AND. CITY='San Diego').
.NOT.	A condition is not true (DO WHILE .NOT. EOF).
.OR.	One or another of two conditions is true (LIST FOR CITY='San Diego' .OR. CITY='Los Angeles').
/	Divides two numbers (? 10/5).
;	Splits and centers headings in report headings (Appendix C; dBASE II Vocabulary).

Command	Definition
<	Less than (LIST FOR LNAME < 'Smith'). Also used to left-justify REPORT headings.
< =	Less than or equal to (LIST FOR LNAME < = 'Smith').
=	Equal to (LIST FOR LNAME = 'Smith').
>	Greater than (LIST FOR LNAME > 'Appleby'). Also used to right-justify REPORT headings.
> =	Greater than or equal to (LIST FOR DATE >= '03/01/83').
?	Displays the contents of a field, memory variable, or the results of a mathematical equation (? 1 + 1).
@	Formats screen and printer displays (@ 5,1 SAY 'Hi').
ACCEPT	Displays a prompt on the screen and waits for a response. Stores answer to a memory variable as character data (ACCEPT 'Do you want more?' TO YN).
ALL	Refers to all records in the data base (DISPLAY ALL, DELETE ALL, REPLACE ALL).
APPEND	Allows us to add new data to our data base.
APPEND FROM	Reads the records from another data base into the data base in use. Adds new records to the bottom of the data base in use (APPEND FROM TEMP).
B:	Signifies drive B for storing data files (CREATE B:MAIL).
BROWSE	Displays a "screenful" of the data base and allows us to scan and make changes to the data base.
COMMAND	Creates or edits a command file (MODIFY COMMAND B:MENU).

Command	Definition
CONTINUE	Used with the LOCATE command to find the next record with a particular characteristic.
COPY	Copies the contents of one data base into another data base (COPY TO TEMP).
COUNT	Counts the records in a data base (COUNT FOR DATE = '03/01/83').
CREATE	Allows us to create a data base, and define its structure (CREATE MAIL).
DATE( )	Displays dBASE 'internal' date [i.e. ? DATE()].
DEBUG	A debugging aid which displays echoed command lines to the printer (SET DEBUG ON).
DEFAULT	Changes the default drive for storing data files (SET DEFAULT TO B).
DELETE	Marks a record for deletion (DELETE RECORD 7).
DELIMITED	Copies dBASE data bases to other data file formats (COPY TO MM.TXT DELIMITED WITH ,).
DESCENDING	Used with SORT to sort from largest to smallest, rather than smallest to largest (SORT ON ZIP TO B:TEMP DESCENDING).
DISPLAY	Shows information about a data base, or its contents (DISPLAY ALL, DISPLAY STRUCTURE).
DO	Runs a command file (DO B:MAIL).
DO WHILE	Used with ENDDO to set up a loop in a command file (DO WHILE .NOT. EOF).
ECHO	A debugging aid, displays all statements in a command file as processed (SET ECHO ON).
EDIT	Displays existing data in a record and allows us to change its contents (EDIT 17).

Command	Definition
ENDDO	Used with the DO WHILE command to mark the bottom of a loop in a command file.
ENDIF	Marks the end of an IF clause in a command file.
EOF	End of File. Used primarily in DO WHILE loops in command files (DO WHILE .NOT. EOF).
ERASE	Clears the screen.
EXACT	Determines how searches will function (SET EXACT ON).
FIELD	Refers to individual fields in a record (CHANGE FIELD...).
FILE	Refers to a disk file. DELETE FILE deletes a disk file. DISPLAY FILE shows disk files.
GET	Used with the READ command to accept field and memory variable data from the screen (@ 5,1 SAY 'Last name' GET LNAME).
GO BOTTOM	Goes to the last record in a data base.
GO TOP	Starts at the first record in a data base.
IF	Determines whether or not to perform commands in a command file based upon some criteria (IF ZIP='92122').
INDEX	Creates an index file of sorted data, (INDEX ON LNAME TO NAMES), or uses an existing index to display data in sorted order (USE B:MAIL INDEX B:NAMES).
INPUT	Displays a prompt on the screen, and waits for a response. Used with numeric data (INPUT 'How many labels per page ' TO PER:PAGE).

Command	Definition
JOIN	Creates a third data base based upon the contents of two existing data bases (JOIN TO B:NEWDB FOR CODE = S.CODE).
LINKAGE	Treats two separate data bases as one (SET LINKAGE ON).
LIST	Shows the contents of a data base.
LIST FOR	Lists data that have some characteristic in common (LIST FOR LNAME = 'Smith').
LOCATE	Finds a record with a particular characteristic (LOCATE FOR LNAME = 'Smith').
MEMORY	Displays memory variables in RAM (DISPLAY MEMORY).
MODIFY	Changes a data base's structure, or creates/edits a command file (MODIFY STRUCTURE, MODIFY COMMAND B:MENU).
OFF	Leaves record numbers out of displays (LIST OFF). Also, turns off parameters (SET PRINT OFF).
ON	Sets dBASE parameters into 'on' mode (SET PRINT ON).
P.	Used with multiple data files to indicate primary field (? P.DATE).
PACK	Permanently deletes records marked for deletion from the data base.
PICTURE	Used with the GET command to make templates and define acceptable character types [@ 12,1 SAY 'Phone number' GET PHONE PICTURE '(999) 999-9999'].
PRINT	Sends displays to the printer (SET PRINT ON, REPORT FORM BYNAME TO PRINT).
QUIT	Exits dBASE II back to the operating system's A> prompt.

Command	Definition
READ	Used with @, SAY, and GET to read in field- and memory-variable data from the screen.
RECALL	Brings back a record marked for deletion (RECALL RECORD 14).
RECORD	Refers to a single record (DELETE RECORD 4).
REPLACE	Changes the current contents of a field with new data. Used in global deletes (REPLACE ALL LNAME WITH 'Smith' FOR LNAME = 'SMITH').
REPORT FORM	Allows us to either create a report format, or display data in a report format (REPORT FORM B:BYNAME).
RETURN	Returns control from a command file to the dot prompt or another command file.
S.	Refers to secondary field (? S.DATE).
SAY	Used with @ to position output on the screen or printer (@ 5,2 SAY 'Hi').
SDF	Standard Data Format. Copies dBASE files to other data base formats (COPY TO BASIC. DAT SDF FOR # < 100).
SELECT PRIMARY	When working with two data bases at once, designates one as the primary data base.
SELECT SECONDARY	When using multiple data files, defines the data base as secondary.
SET	Changes a dBASE II parameter (SET TALK ON).
SKIP	Skips to the next record in the data base. Can also skip more or less than one record (SKIP 10, SKIP −3).
SORT	Rearranges records on a data base into sorted order. Requires that records be sorted to another data base (SORT ON LNAME TO B:TEMP).

Command	Definition
STEP	A debugging aid, which pauses after each line in a command file is processed (SET STEP ON).
STORE	Stores a value to a memory variable (STORE 1 TO COUNTER).
STR	Changes numeric data to strings [STORE STR (CNTR,2) TO SCNTR].
STRUCTURE	Refers to the structure, rather than the contents of a data base (DISPLAY STRUCTURE).
SUM	Adds a column of fields, and displays the total (SUM AMOUNT).
TALK	Sets dBASE's miscellaneous messages on or off (SET TALK OFF).
TOTAL	Summarizes and totals a data base to another data base. File must be either presorted or preindexed (TOTAL ON CODE TO B:SALESUMM).
TRIM	Removes trailing blanks from a field's contents [LIST TRIM(FNAME),LNAME].
UPDATE	Revises the file in use by adding or replacing data from another data base (UPDATE ON CODE FROM B:SALES ADD QTY REPLACE PRICE).
USE	Tells dBASE which data base to work with (USE B:MAIL).
VAL	Changes character strings to numerics [? VAL(ADDRESS)].
WAIT	Stops execution of a command file, and waits for user to press a key. The key press is stored to a memory variable (WAIT TO DATA).

Index

The SYBEX Library

Buyer's Guide

THE BEST OF TI 99/4A™ CARTRIDGES
by Thomas Blackadar
150 pp., illustr., Ref. 0-137
Save yourself time and frustration when buying TI 99/4A software. This buyer's guide gives an overview of the best available programs, with information on how to set up the computer to run them.

FAMILY COMPUTERS UNDER $200
by Doug Mosher
160 pp., illustr., Ref. 0-149
Find out what these inexpensive machines can do for you and your family. "If you're just getting started . . . this is the book to read before you buy."—Richard O'Reilly, Los Angeles newspaper columnist

PORTABLE COMPUTERS
by Sheldon Crop and Doug Mosher
128 pp., illustr., Ref. 0-144
"This book provides a clear and concise introduction to the expanding new world of personal computers."—Mark Powelson, Editor, *San Francisco Focus Magazine*

THE BEST OF VIC-20™ SOFTWARE
by Thomas Blackadar
150 pp., illustr., Ref. 0-139
Save yourself time and frustration with this buyer's guide to VIC-20 software. Find the best game, music, education, and home management programs on the market today.

SELECTING THE RIGHT DATA BASE SOFTWARE
SELECTING THE RIGHT WORD PROCESSING SOFTWARE
SELECTING THE RIGHT SPREADSHEET SOFTWARE
by Kathy McHugh and Veronica Corchado
80 pp., illustr., Ref. 0-174, 0-177, 0-178
This series on selecting the right business software offers the busy professional concise, informative reviews of the best available software packages.

Introduction to Computers

OVERCOMING COMPUTER FEAR
by Jeff Berner
112 pp., illustr., Ref. 0-145
This easy-going introduction to computers helps you separate the facts from the myths.

COMPUTER ABC'S
by Daniel Le Noury and Rodnay Zaks
64 pp., illustr., Ref. 0-167
This beautifully illustrated, colorful book for parents and children takes you alphabetically through the world of computers, explaining each concept in simple language.

PARENTS, KIDS, AND COMPUTERS
by Lynn Alpers and Meg Holmberg
208 pp., illustr., Ref. 0-151
This book answers your questions about the educational possibilities of home computers.

THE COLLEGE STUDENT'S COMPUTER HANDBOOK
by Bryan Pfaffenberger
350 pp., illustr., Ref. 0-170
This friendly guide will aid students in selecting a computer system for college study, managing information in a college course, and writing research papers.

COMPUTER CRAZY
by Daniel Le Noury
100 pp., illustr., Ref. 0-173
No matter how you feel about computers, these cartoons will have you laughing about them.

DON'T!
(or How to Care for Your Computer)
by Rodnay Zaks
214pp., 100 illustr., Ref. 0-065
The correct way to handle and care for all elements of a computer system, including what to do when something doesn't work.

YOUR FIRST COMPUTER
by Rodnay Zaks
258 pp., 150 illustr., Ref. 0-045
The most popular introduction to small computers and their peripherals: what they do and how to buy one.

INTERNATIONAL MICROCOMPUTER DICTIONARY
120 pp., Ref. 0-067
All the definitions and acronyms of micro-computer jargon defined in a handy pocket-sized edition. Includes translations of the most popular terms into ten languages.

FROM CHIPS TO SYSTEMS: AN INTRODUCTION TO MICROPROCESSORS
by Rodnay Zaks
552 pp., 400 illustr., Ref. 0-063
A simple and comprehensive introduction to microprocessors from both a hardware and software standpoint: what they are, how they operate, how to assemble them into a complete system.

Personal Computers

ATARI

YOUR FIRST ATARI® PROGRAM
by Rodnay Zaks
150 pp., illustr., Ref. 0-130
A fully illustrated, easy-to-use introduction to ATARI BASIC programming. Will have the reader programming in a matter of hours.

BASIC EXERCISES FOR THE ATARI®
by J.P. Lamoitier
251 pp., illustr., Ref. 0-101
Teaches ATARI BASIC through actual practice using graduated exercises drawn from everyday applications.

THE EASY GUIDE TO YOUR ATARI® 600XL/800XL
by Thomas Blackadar
175 pp., illustr., Ref. 0-125
This jargon-free companion will help you get started on the right foot with your new 600XL or 800XL ATARI computer.

ATARI® BASIC PROGRAMS IN MINUTES
by Stanley R. Trost
170 pp., illustr., Ref. 0-143
You can use this practical set of programs without any prior knowledge of BASIC! Application examples are taken from a wide variety of fields, including business, home management, and real estate.

Commodore 64/VIC-20

THE COMMODORE 64™/VIC-20™ BASIC HANDBOOK
by Douglas Hergert

144 pp., illustr., Ref. 0-116

A complete listing with descriptions and instructive examples of each of the Commodore 64 BASIC keywords and functions. A handy reference guide, organized like a dictionary.

THE EASY GUIDE TO YOUR COMMODORE 64™
by Joseph Kascmer

160 pp., illustr., Ref. 0-129

A friendly introduction to using the Commodore 64.

YOUR FIRST VIC-20™ PROGRAM
by Rodnay Zaks

150 pp., illustr., Ref. 0-129

A fully illustrated, easy-to-use introduction to VIC-20 BASIC programming. Will have the reader programming in a matter of hours.

THE VIC-20™ CONNECTION
by James W. Coffron

260 pp., 120 illustr., Ref. 0-128

Teaches elementary interfacing and BASIC programming of the VIC-20 for connection to external devices and household appliances.

YOUR FIRST COMMODORE 64™ PROGRAM
by Rodnay Zaks

182 pp., illustr., Ref. 0-172

You can learn to write simple programs without any prior knowledge of mathematics or computers! Guided by colorful illustrations and step-by-step instructions, you'll be constructing programs within an hour or two.

COMMODORE 64™ BASIC PROGRAMS IN MINUTES
by Stanley R. Trost

170 pp., illustr., Ref. 0-154

Here is a practical set of programs for business, finance, real estate, data analysis, record keeping and educational applications.

GRAPHICS GUIDE TO THE COMMODORE 64™
by Charles Platt

192 pp., illustr., Ref. 0-138

This easy-to-understand book will appeal to anyone who wants to master the Commodore 64's powerful graphics features.

IBM

THE ABC'S OF THE IBM® PC
by Joan Lasselle and Carol Ramsay

100 pp., illustr., Ref. 0-102

This is the book that will take you through the first crucial steps in learning to use the IBM PC.

THE BEST OF IBM® PC SOFTWARE
by Stanley R. Trost

144 pp., illustr., Ref. 0-104

Separates the wheat from the chaff in the world of IBM PC software. Tells you what to expect from the best available IBM PC programs.

THE IBM® PC-DOS HANDBOOK
by Richard Allen King

144 pp., illustr., Ref. 0-103

Explains the PC disk operating system, giving the user better control over the system. Get the most out of your PC by adapting its capabilities to your specific needs.

BUSINESS GRAPHICS FOR THE IBM® PC
by Nelson Ford

200 pp., illustr., Ref. 0-124

Ready-to-run programs for creating line graphs, complex illustrative multiple bar graphs, picture graphs, and more. An ideal way to use your PC's business capabilities!

THE IBM® PC CONNECTION
by James W. Coffron
200 pp., illustr., Ref. 0-127
Teaches elementary interfacing and BASIC programming of the IBM PC for connection to external devices and household appliances.

BASIC EXERCISES FOR THE IBM® PERSONAL COMPUTER
by J.P. Lamoitier
252 pp., 90 illustr., Ref. 0-088
Teaches IBM BASIC through actual practice, using graduated exercises drawn from everyday applications.

USEFUL BASIC PROGRAMS FOR THE IBM® PC
by Stanley R. Trost
144 pp., Ref. 0-111
This collection of programs takes full advantage of the interactive capabilities of your IBM Personal Computer. Financial calculations, investment analysis, record keeping, and math practice—made easier on your IBM PC.

YOUR FIRST IBM® PC PROGRAM
by Rodnay Zaks
182 pp., illustr., Ref. 0-171
This well-illustrated book makes programming easy for children and adults.

YOUR IBM® PC JUNIOR
by Douglas Hergert
250 pp., illustr., Ref. 0-179
This comprehensive reference guide to IBM's most economical microcomputer offers many practical applications and all the helpful information you'll need to get started with your IBM PC Junior.

DATA FILE PROGRAMMING ON YOUR IBM® PC
by Alan Simpson
275 pp., illustr., Ref. 0-146
This book provides instructions and examples of managing data files in BASIC. Programming designs and developments are extensively discussed.

Apple

THE EASY GUIDE TO YOUR APPLE II®
by Joseph Kascmer
160 pp., illustr., Ref. 0-122
A friendly introduction to using the Apple II, II plus and the new IIe.

BASIC EXERCISES FOR THE APPLE®
by J.P. Lamoitier
250 pp., 90 illustr., Ref. 0-084
Teaches Apple BASIC through actual practice, using graduated exercises drawn from everyday applications.

APPLE II® BASIC HANDBOOK
by Douglas Hergert
144 pp., illustr., Ref. 0-155
A complete listing with descriptions and instructive examples of each of the Apple II BASIC keywords and functions. A handy reference guide, organized like a dictionary.

APPLE II® BASIC PROGRAMS IN MINUTES
by Stanley R. Trost
150 pp., illustr., Ref. 0-121
A collection of ready-to-run programs for financial calculations, investment analysis, record keeping, and many more home and office applications. These programs can be entered on your Apple II plus or IIe in minutes!

YOUR FIRST APPLE II® PROGRAM
by Rodnay Zaks
150 pp., illustr., Ref. 0-136
A fully illustrated, easy-to-use introduction to APPLE BASIC programming. Will have the reader programming in a matter of hours.

THE APPLE® CONNECTION
by James W. Coffron
264 pp., 120 illustr., Ref. 0-085
Teaches elementary interfacing and BASIC programming of the Apple for connection to external devices and household appliances.

TRS-80

YOUR COLOR COMPUTER
by Doug Mosher
350 pp., illustr., Ref. 0-097
Patience and humor guide the reader through purchasing, setting up, programming, and using the Radio Shack TRS-80/TDP Series 100 Color Computer. A complete introduction.

THE FOOLPROOF GUIDE TO SCRIPSIT™ WORD PROCESSING
by Jeff Berner
225 pp., illustr., Ref. 0-098
Everything you need to know about SCRIPSIT—from starting out, to mastering document editing. This user-friendly guide is written in plain English, with a touch of wit.

Timex/Sinclair 1000/ZX81

YOUR TIMEX/SINCLAIR 1000 AND ZX81™
by Douglas Hergert
159 pp., illustr., Ref. 0-099
This book explains the set-up, operation, and capabilities of the Timex/Sinclair 1000 and ZX81. Includes how to interface peripheral devices, and introduces BASIC programming.

THE TIMEX/SINCLAIR 1000™ BASIC HANDBOOK
by Douglas Hergert
170 pp., illustr., Ref. 0-113
A complete alphabetical listing with explanations and examples of each word in the T/S 1000 BASIC vocabulary; will allow you quick, error-free programming of your T/S 1000.

TIMEX/SINCLAIR 1000™ BASIC PROGRAMS IN MINUTES
by Stanley R. Trost
150 pp., illustr., Ref. 0-119
A collection of ready-to-run programs for financial calculations, investment analysis, record keeping, and many more home and office applications. These programs can be entered on your T/S 1000 in minutes!

MORE USES FOR YOUR TIMEX/SINCLAIR 1000™
Astronomy on Your Computer
by Eric Burgess
176 pp., illustr., Ref. 0-112
Ready-to-run programs that turn your TV into a planetarium.

Other Popular Computers

YOUR FIRST TI 99/4A™ PROGRAM
by Rodnay Zaks
182 pp., illustr., Ref. 0-157
Colorfully illustrated, this book concentrates on the essentials of programming in a clear, entertaining fashion.

THE RADIO SHACK® NOTEBOOK COMPUTER
by Orson Kellogg
128 pp., illustr., Ref. 0-150
Whether you already have the Radio Shack Model 100 notebook computer, or are interested in buying one, this book will clearly explain what it can do for you.

THE EASY GUIDE TO YOUR COLECO ADAM™
by Thomas Blackadar
175 pp., illustr., Ref. 0-181
This quick reference guide shows you how to get started on your Coleco Adam with a minimum of technical jargon.

YOUR KAYPRO II/4/10™
by Andrea Reid and Gary Deidrichs
250 pp., illustr., Ref. 0-166
This book is a non-technical introduction to the KAYPRO family of computers. You will find all you need to know about operating your KAYPRO within this one complete guide.

Software and Applications

Operating Systems

THE CP/M® HANDBOOK
by Rodnay Zaks
320 pp., 100 illustr., Ref 0-048
An indispensable reference and guide to CP/M—the most widely-used operating system for small computers.

MASTERING CP/M®
by Alan R. Miller
398 pp., illustr., Ref. 0-068
For advanced CP/M users or systems programmers who want maximum use of the CP/M operating system . . . takes up where our *CP/M Handbook* leaves off.

THE BEST OF CP/M® SOFTWARE
by John D. Halamka
250 pp., illustr., Ref. 0-100
This book reviews tried-and-tested, commercially available software for your CP/M system.

REAL WORLD UNIX™
by John D. Halamka
250 pp., illustr., Ref. 0-093
This book is written for the beginning and intermediate UNIX user in a practical, straightforward manner, with specific instructions given for many special applications.

THE CP/M PLUS™ HANDBOOK
by Alan R. Miller
250 pp., illustr., Ref. 0-158
This guide is easy for the beginner to understand, yet contains valuable information for advanced users of CP/M Plus (Version 3).

Business Software

INTRODUCTION TO WORDSTAR™
by Arthur Naiman
202 pp., 30 illustr., Ref. 0-077
Makes it easy to learn how to use WordStar, a powerful word processing program for personal computers.

PRACTICAL WORDSTAR™ USES
by Julie Anne Arca
200 pp., illustr., Ref. 0-107
Pick your most time-consuming office tasks and this book will show you how to streamline them with WordStar.

MASTERING VISICALC®
by Douglas Hergert
217 pp., 140 illustr., Ref. 0-090
Explains how to use the VisiCalc "electronic spreadsheet" functions and provides examples of each. Makes using this powerful program simple.

DOING BUSINESS WITH VISICALC®
by Stanley R. Trost
260 pp., Ref. 0-086
Presents accounting and management planning applications—from financial statements to master budgets; from pricing models to investment strategies.

DOING BUSINESS WITH SUPERCALC™
by Stanley R. Trost
248 pp., illustr., Ref. 0-095
Presents accounting and management planning applications—from financial statements to master budgets; from pricing models to investment strategies.

VISICALC® FOR SCIENCE AND ENGINEERING
by Stanley R. Trost and Charles Pomernacki
225 pp., illustr., Ref. 0-096
More than 50 programs for solving technical problems in the science and engineering fields. Applications range from math

and statistics to electrical and electronic engineering.

DOING BUSINESS WITH 1-2-3™
by Stanley R. Trost
250 pp., illustr., Ref. 0-159
If you are a business professional using the 1-2-3 software package, you will find the spreadsheet and graphics models provided in this book easy to use "as is" in everyday business situations.

THE ABC'S OF 1-2-3™
by Chris Gilbert
225 pp., illustr., Ref. 0-168
For those new to the LOTUS 1-2-3 program, this book offers step-by-step instructions in mastering its spreadsheet, data base, and graphing capabilities.

DOING BUSINESS WITH dBASE II™
by Stanley R. Trost
250 pp., illustr., Ref. 0-160
Learn to use dBASE II for accounts receivable, recording business income and expenses, keeping personal records and mailing lists, and much more.

DOING BUSINESS WITH MULTIPLAN™
by Richard Allen King and Stanley R. Trost
250 pp., illustr., Ref. 0-148
This book will show you how using Multiplan can be nearly as easy as learning to use a pocket calculator. It presents a collection of templates that can be applied "as is" to business situations.

DOING BUSINESS WITH PFS®
by Stanley R. Trost
250 pp., illustr., Ref. 0-161
This practical guide describes specific business and personal applications in detail. Learn to use PFS for accounting, data analysis, mailing lists and more.

INFOPOWER: PRACTICAL INFOSTAR™ USES
by Jule Anne Arca and Charles F. Pirro
275 pp., illustr., Ref. 0-108
This book gives you an overview of Info-Star, including DataStar and ReportStar, WordStar, MailMerge, and SuperSort. Hands on exercises take you step-by-step through real life business applications.

WRITING WITH EASYWRITER II™
by Douglas W. Topham
250 pp., illustr., Ref. 0-141
Friendly style, handy illustrations, and numerous sample exercises make it easy to learn the EasyWriter II word processing system.

Business Applications

INTRODUCTION TO WORD PROCESSING
by Hal Glatzer
205 pp., 140 illustr., Ref. 0-076
Explains in plain language what a word processor can do, how it improves productivity, how to use a word processor and how to buy one wisely.

COMPUTER POWER FOR YOUR LAW OFFICE
by Daniel Remer
225 pp., Ref. 0-109
How to use computers to reach peak productivity in your law office, simply and inexpensively.

OFFICE EFFICIENCY WITH PERSONAL COMPUTERS
by Sheldon Crop
175 pp., illustr., Ref. 0-165
Planning for computerization of your office? This book provides a simplified discussion of the challenges involved for everyone from business owner to clerical worker.

COMPUTER POWER FOR YOUR ACCOUNTING OFFICE
by James Morgan
250 pp., illustr., Ref. 0-164
This book is a convenient source of information about computerizing you accounting office, with an emphasis on hardware and software options.

Languages

C

UNDERSTANDING C
by Bruce Hunter
200 pp., Ref 0-123
Explains how to use the powerful C language for a variety of applications. Some programming experience assumed.

FIFTY C PROGRAMS
by Bruce Hunter
200 pp., illustr., Ref. 0-155
Beginning as well as intermediate C programmers will find this a useful guide to programming techniques and specific applications.

BUSINESS PROGRAMS IN C
by Leon Wortman and Thomas O. Sidebottom
200 pp., illustr., Ref. 0-153
This book provides source code listings of C programs for the business person or experienced programmer. Each easy-to-follow tutorial applies directly to a business situation.

BASIC

YOUR FIRST BASIC PROGRAM
by Rodnay Zaks
150pp. illustr. in color, Ref. 0-129
A "how-to-program" book for the first time computer user, aged 8 to 88.

FIFTY BASIC EXERCISES
by J. P. Lamoitier
232 pp., 90 illustr., Ref. 0-056
Teaches BASIC by actual practice, using graduated exercises drawn from everyday applications. All programs written in Microsoft BASIC.

INSIDE BASIC GAMES
by Richard Mateosian
348 pp., 120 illustr., Ref. 0-055
Teaches interactive BASIC programming through games. Games are written in Microsoft BASIC and can run on the TRS-80, Apple II and PET/CBM.

BASIC FOR BUSINESS
by Douglas Hergert
224 pp., 15 illustr., Ref. 0-080
A logically organized, no-nonsense introduction to BASIC programming for business applications. Includes many fully-explained accounting programs, and shows you how to write them.

EXECUTIVE PLANNING WITH BASIC
by X. T. Bui
196 pp., 19 illustr., Ref. 0-083
An important collection of business management decision models in BASIC, including Inventory Management (EOQ), Critical Path Analysis and PERT, Financial Ratio Analysis, Portfolio Management, and much more.

BASIC PROGRAMS FOR SCIENTISTS AND ENGINEERS
by Alan R. Miller
318 pp., 120 illustr., Ref. 0-073
This book from the "Programs for Scientists and Engineers" series provides a library of problem-solving programs while developing proficiency in BASIC.

CELESTIAL BASIC
by Eric Burgess
300 pp., 65 illustr., Ref. 0-087
A collection of BASIC programs that rapidly complete the chores of typical astronomical computations. It's like having a planetarium in your own home! Displays apparent movement of stars, planets and meteor showers.

YOUR SECOND BASIC PROGRAM

by Gary Lippman

250 pp., illustr., Ref. 0-152

A sequel to *Your First BASIC Program*, this book follows the same patient, detailed approach and brings you to the next level of programming skill.

Pascal

INTRODUCTION TO PASCAL (Including UCSD Pascal™)

by Rodnay Zaks

420 pp., 130 illustr., Ref. 0-066

A step-by-step introduction for anyone wanting to learn the Pascal language. Describes UCSD and Standard Pascals. No technical background is assumed.

THE PASCAL HANDBOOK

by Jacques Tiberghien

486 pp., 270 illustr., Ref. 0-053

A dictionary of the Pascal language, defining every reserved word, operator, procedure and function found in all major versions of Pascal.

APPLE® PASCAL GAMES

by Douglas Hergert and Joseph T. Kalash

372 pp., 40 illustr., Ref. 0-074

A collection of the most popular computer games in Pascal, challenging the reader not only to play but to investigate how games are implemented on the computer.

INTRODUCTION TO THE UCSD p-SYSTEM™

by Charles W. Grant and Jon Butah

300 pp., 10 illustr., Ref. 0-061

A simple, clear introduction to the UCSD Pascal Operating System; for beginners through experienced programmers.

PASCAL PROGRAMS FOR SCIENTISTS AND ENGINEERS

by Alan R. Miller

374 pp., 120 illustr., Ref. 0-058

A comprehensive collection of frequently used algorithms for scientific and technical applications, programmed in Pascal.

Includes such programs as curve-fitting, integrals and statistical techniques.

DOING BUSINESS WITH PASCAL

by Richard Hergert and Douglas Hergert

371 pp., illustr., Ref. 0-091

Practical tips for using Pascal in business programming. Includes design considerations, language extensions, and applications examples.

Assembly Language Programming

PROGRAMMING THE 6502

by Rodnay Zaks

386 pp., 160 illustr., Ref. 0-046

Assembly language programming for the 6502, from basic concepts to advanced data structures.

6502 APPLICATIONS

by Rodnay Zaks

278 pp., 200 illustr., Ref. 0-015

Real-life application techniques: the input/output book for the 6502.

ADVANCED 6502 PROGRAMMING

by Rodnay Zaks

292 pp., 140 illustr., Ref. 0-089

Third in the 6502 series. Teaches more advanced programming techniques, using games as a framework for learning.

PROGRAMMING THE Z80

by Rodnay Zaks

624 pp., 200 illustr., Ref. 0-069

A complete course in programming the Z80 microprocessor and a thorough introduction to assembly language.

Z80 APPLICATIONS

by James W. Coffron

288 pp., illustr., Ref. 0-094

Covers techniques and applications for using peripheral devices with a Z80 based system.

PROGRAMMING THE 6809
by Rodnay Zaks and William Labiak
362 pp., 150 illustr., Ref. 0-078
This book explains how to program the 6809 in assembly language. No prior programming knowledge required.

PROGRAMMING THE Z8000
by Richard Mateosian
298 pp., 124 illustr., Ref. 0-032
How to program the Z8000 16-bit microprocessor. Includes a description of the architecture and function of the Z8000 and its family of support chips.

PROGRAMMING THE 8086/8088
by James W. Coffron
300 pp., illustr., Ref. 0-120
This book explains how to program the 8086 and 8088 in assembly language. No prior programming knowledge required.

Other Languages

FORTRAN PROGRAMS FOR SCIENTISTS AND ENGINEERS
by Alan R. Miller
280 pp., 120 illustr., Ref. 0-082
In the "Programs for Scientists and Engineers" series, this book provides specific scientific and engineering application programs written in FORTRAN.

A MICROPROGRAMMED APL IMPLEMENTATION
by Rodnay Zaks
350 pp., Ref. 0-005
An expert-level text presenting the complete conceptual analysis and design of an APL interpreter, and actual listing of the microcode.

Hardware and Peripherals

MICROPROCESSOR INTERFACING TECHNIQUES
by Rodnay Zaks and Austin Lesea
456 pp., 400 illustr., Ref. 0-029
Complete hardware and software interconnect techniques, including D to A conversion, peripherals, standard buses and troubleshooting.

THE RS-232 SOLUTION
by Joe Campbell
225 pp., illustr., Ref. 0-140
Finally, a book that will show you how to correctly interface your computer to any RS-232-C peripheral.

USING CASSETTE RECORDERS WITH COMPUTERS
by James Richard Cook
175 pp., illustr., Ref. 0-169
Whatever your computer or application, you will find this book helpful in explaining details of cassette care and maintenance.

 **SYBEX** COMPUTER BOOKS

are different.

Here is why . . .

At SYBEX, each book is designed with you in mind. Every manuscript is carefully selected and supervised by our editors, who are themselves computer experts. We publish the best authors, whose technical expertise is matched by an ability to write clearly and to communicate effectively. Programs are thoroughly tested for accuracy by our technical staff. Our computerized production department goes to great lengths to make sure that each book is well-designed.

In the pursuit of timeliness, SYBEX has achieved many publishing firsts. SYBEX was among the first to integrate personal computers used by authors and staff into the publishing process. SYBEX was the first to publish books on the CP/M operating system, microprocessor interfacing techniques, word processing, and many more topics.

Expertise in computers and dedication to the highest quality product have made SYBEX a world leader in computer book publishing. Translated into fourteen languages, SYBEX books have helped millions of people around the world to get the most from their computers. We hope we have helped you, too.

For a complete catalog of our publications please contact:

U.S.A.	FRANCE	GERMANY
SYBEX, Inc.	SYBEX	SYBEX-VERLAG
2344 Sixth Street	4 Place Félix-Eboué	Heyestr. 22
Berkeley,	75583 Paris Cedex 12	4000 Düsseldorf 12
California 94710	France	West Germany
Tel: (800) 227-2346	Tel: 1/347-30-20	Tel: (0211) 287066
(415) 848-8233	Telex: 211801	Telex: 08 588 163
Telex: 336311		